AS YEARS GO BY

AS YEARS GO BY

the 60s revolution at British Decca

Photographs by David Wedgbury
Commentary by John Tracy

Foreword by Tim Rice

PAVILION

Dedicated to the spirit
that was Decca

First published in Great Britain
in 1993 by
PAVILION BOOKS LIMITED
196 Shaftesbury Avenue,
London WC2H 8JL

Photographs copyright
© David Wedgbury 1993
Text copyright
© John Tracy 1993
Foreword copyright
© Tim Rice 1993

Designed by Andrew Barron &
Collis Clements Associates

A CIP catalogue record for this book is
available from the British Library

ISBN 1 85145 007 X

Printed and bound in Italy
by Arnoldo Mondadori

2 4 6 8 10 9 7 5 3 1

Companion CD and MC *As Years Go
By* are available on Deram via PolyGram:
CD 844 014–2; MC 844 014–4.

David Wedgbury would like to
acknowledge the assistance of
Vincent Eckersley, Roger Blake and
photographic printer John Roffey

Page 2: The Cavern, Liverpool.
Page 5: The Who.
Page 6: Tim Rice.
Page 7: The Rolling Stones.
Page 8: David Wedgbury.
Page 9: The Checkmates.
Page 11: Donovan, Twinkle and
Jimmy Savile

Foreword

You can almost hear David Wedgbury's photographs in this fascinating portfolio. Some pictures rightly became famous; some have rarely, if ever, been exposed to the public gaze before. All come with their own soundtrack which everyone who first listened to pop music in the Fifties or Sixties will recreate as they wander through the images herein and relearn the anecdotes John Tracy recalls.

There is no point in beating around the bush; the Sixties were the golden age in British popular culture. This is not just the romantic rambling of a middle-aged observer, it is an incontrovertible fact.

Led by the incomparable Beatles, in turn barely a B-side ahead of the Rolling Stones and a host of other confident and charmed performers, the singers and songwriters that roared out of every corner of the kingdom from late 1962 until an unidentified moment around the end of 1968, were magnificent and matchless. The Americans, with a few exceptions, were caught on the back foot.

The hit-makers of the Seventies and Eighties had their moments, some glorious, but they never seemed part of some stupendous movement, stretching way beyond mere music, that affected us all – they had less to discover, they knew too much. They did not have to come up with a great new single every three months or die. They were encouraged to indulge themselves on long-winded albums, stretching themselves beyond their capabilities. In 1993 children were spending more on electronic games than on music.

At Decca, David Wedgbury photographed virtually every British act the company signed in the Sixties and a slew of visiting Americans. Not all were gifted, not all were unforgettable, but they were all part of the whole. They looked good. If you were around at the time, enough said. If you weren't, enough can never be said.

TIM RICE 1993

Preface

In the world of pop music, before the advent of the now familiar promotional video, the 10" × 8" black and white glossy artist photograph reigned supreme as the principal means of artists' promotion. The 10" × 8" glossy, coupled with an artist's biography, usually a pretentious list of the artist's influences, likes and dislikes, was used through press distribution to familiarize the pop fans with the images of the record makers.

Decca Records was early to recognize the value of photography in the promotion of its music business, and established a small studio in the late 1950s with one photographer and a dark room assistant. The 60s pop explosion brought increased demands for photography and by 1963 the studio had grown into a department employing twelve staff.

I headed the photographic department through the 60s working with an assistant. The remaining staff were employed in the processing and production of vast quantities of black and white prints up to 20" × 30" in size for press, promotion and for record store display.

The Decca studio was located at Black Prince Road in Lambeth, in a high-ceilinged Victorian building formerly owned by the Doulton Pottery. The building was used as an annexe to the Decca head office building on the Albert Embankment. In addition to photography it also housed an art studio and a variety of other odd bods that were probably best not seen in the marbled halls of the main building, which boasted almost its own regiment of uniformed commissionaires.

The work of our department did much to establish and influence the emerging art of pop photography. This collection of photographs is dedicated to the spirit of the time and to the spirit that was Decca.

DAVID WEDGBURY 1993

Introduction

Although, from the official 'date-on-the-calendar' angle, the 1960s began on 1 January 1960, to all intents and purposes the action-packed era which is referred to as the 'Swinging Sixties' didn't even last a decade. No, 'it' began in October 1962 when four Liverpool lads named the Beatles issued a modest little pop song they'd written called *Love Me Do*.

Although destined only to peak at an unspectacular No. 17 in Britain during December and, at the time do nothing in the hallowed US marketplace, it manifested a watershed in musical and social history. As the New Year was ushered in, a youth revolution simultaneously also arrived whose knock-on effect would exceed anything previously encountered. So irresistible was its power, the 'establishment' never regained ground and Britain, for so long in matters of entertainment America's slavish imitator, suddenly, and unexpectedly, found itself the world's pacemaker.

During the post-war mid-Fifties Bill Haley and Elvis Presley-inspired rock 'n' roll had given rebellious youth its first modern voice, but by 1960 those primal screams had been strangled. Haley, once physically viewed, could be seen as one of 'them' (i.e. adult) masquerading as one of 'us'; Elvis had been inducted into the Army and would come back with his melodic 'rough edges' knocked off. Excellent though they were, *Wooden Heart* and *Are You Lonesome Tonight* were a far cry from *Jailhouse Rock* and *Hard Headed Woman*; Little Richard and Jerry Lee Lewis's sales were seriously waning; the Everly Brothers and Ricky Nelson were never that kind of wild anyway, proved highly adaptable, and audiences old and new grew with them.

Every case could be examined separately, but America's record companies around 1960 had again taken the initiative as taste arbiters and introduced the likes of 'sanitized' pop through Frankie Avalon, Bobby Rydell and hundreds more. Then came the Beatles, pursued by innumerable other British groups, and pop music was turned on its head worldwide within eighteen months.

Nobody could have planned what happened from the outset, but the active music scenes of such major British cities as Liverpool, Birmingham, Newcastle, Manchester, Glasgow and London, aided and abetted by Germany's sweaty Hamburg and Hannover clubs where so many aspiring UK acts went to ply their trade, were an 'accident' just waiting to happen. The 'Fab Four' opened Pandora's Box, and all sorts of tricks sprang from within, but most of all a raw energy burst into view which only the mid-to-late Seventies punk

explosion has ever even hoped to emulate. The primary difference though was the Sixties' 'happening' was built on, naively or otherwise, initially a positive fun-to-be-alive basis, while punk emphasized a wholly negative, destructive image.

Back in the Sixties two major capital-based record companies dominated Britain's music industry. From Manchester Square, W1, hailed EMI, calling itself, with some justification, 'The Greatest Recording Organization In The World'. EMI dated from 1931 when three formerly independent labels had grouped together so as to withstand the Depression; it signed the Beatles after twice rejecting them. Its great competitor from 9, Albert Embankment, SE1, beside the River Thames with studios in West Hampstead, was the Decca Record Company, brainchild of one man, Edward Lewis, who had opened its doors in 1929. They had let the Liverpool quartet irrevocably slip through their fingers, and thereafter adopted an open Artists and Repertoire (A&R) policy. In a nutshell, if they put their commitment behind enough acts, they'd surely discover one of similar epoch-making properties to that which had got away. They did – the Rolling Stones – but a magnificent treasury of alternative uncut diamonds were also unearthed in the process.

Although they had two other more recent rivals in the Dutch Philips organization and the Fifties-founded Pye Electronics offshoot, between them Decca and EMI controlled not only the British industry, but an enormous part of the rest of the world's, excluding America. The latter had for decades showed only minimal interest in events outside her own huge coastline, leaving Britain's two opportunists the kind of carte blanche openings unbelievable today, and both grasped them gratefully. Naturally, when that Sixties' revolution came, both were perfectly equipped to ensure their initiatives reached every marketplace.

The changes within the period 1963–9 itself were also unprecedented: that new, raw pop/R&B mainstream with matching mop-top haircuts the Beatles pioneered in 1963 had altered out of all recognition four years later. Now the 'idealist' peace and love culture, with its more than liberal sprinkling of drugs, saw suits, collars and ties consigned to the dustbin in favour of beads, kaftans and 'experimental' music. Pop – the singles market – came in for unjustified derision; it was for the kids. Serious 'rock' artists embraced the LP as the only true method of expression, but much of the immediacy, excitement and glamour which had always surrounded all things 'media' was now viewed negatively. 'Commercial' became a dirty word, but still the records sold across a broader youth spectrum.

Having been knocked sideways by the British 'Beat Boom' of 1963–5, America again began to restore the status quo and introduce significant new international stars to replace those who had fallen by the wayside in droves, and although progressively both Decca and EMI found their previous absolute market domination outside the US eroding as their cousins sought 'independence' – the London-American label for Decca and EMI's later-instigated Stateside imprint had flourished through leasing US products almost unhindered from myriad sources for several years – the pair were still impressively situated at the start of the 1970s. Admittedly though, the writing was on the wall at Albert Embankment through the disappearance of such irreplaceable giants as Warner Brothers, RCA and Atlantic.

The 1960s were the years, nevertheless, when popular music 'grew up' and recognized fully its potential impact on social behaviour generally and manipulated, for both better and worse, that situation. The adrenalin which powered so many people into so many diverse projects in such a relatively brief time though was staggering, and it has left a legacy that no subsequent events have managed to eclipse, nor ever will. Above all it was a 'human' era, whereas today's technology places ever greater emphasis on the achievements of the soulless computer and its faceless operators.

Pop, like cinema, was then about personalities, and ubiquitous use of cameras to capture and preserve those who were to present marketable confections to the public masses was essential. Hollywood had long appreciated the power of atmospheric monochrome photographs, and several of those behind the shutter there became almost as well known as their subjects. In the Sixties a handful of British photographers too began to be recognized by their work, such as Harry Hammond, Angus McBean and Gered Mankowitz.

To manufacture an endless supply of illustrations of its global stars for use on disc sleeves, in the company's retailed *Records Magazine* and as a focal point for its extensive promotional activities, Decca UK had set up a studio in the 1950s which expanded as required with the growing importance of its acts in the successive decade. David Wedgbury became the key figure in that department and visually preserved for posterity much of the ever-changing magic that was an integral part of the Decca Group's contribution to pop's historical, ongoing tapestry of sight and sound. His work graces many classic albums.

And my introduction to this wonderful world? The first 78 I ever purchased came from the Decca company. I was five and it was on London-American . . .   JOHN TRACY

Paul Anka

One of the shrewdest performers in the business, and a genuine major talent unlike some of his manufactured rivals, Paul Anka had already sold some thirty million discs when he moved to American RCA from ABC in 1962 – and brought his catalogue with him.

An infant prodigy as a mimic who wrote his own debut worldwide smash, *Diana*, at 15, Anka's international appeal may be measured by the fact that in 1963 a staggering 250,000 plus paying customers watched his stage act over a ten-day booking – in the Philippines!

Once the British beat boom swept America though, Canadian-born Anka's teenage-girl appeal subsided swiftly and thereafter he concentrated on middle-ground albums and launching other artists including Steve Goodman; in the Seventies a matured Paul revived his hits tally with a different variety of female-orientated compositions like *You're Having My Baby*, concurrently with custom-tailoring for others such as Tom Jones (*She's A Lady*) and Frank Sinatra (*My Way*).

Brenda Lee

Aptly nicknamed 'Little Miss Dynamite' – she measured a mere 4 feet 11 inches in height and tipped the scales at an even 100 pounds – you had to *see* this diminutive woman-child to believe such a remarkable voice could emanate from what appeared to be a little girl.

If Nashville-based Brenda (Mae Tarpley) Lee was small in stature she'd been big on disc sales for American Decca since 1956, and gave a whole new meaning to that hackneyed cliché, 'The Show Must Go On'.

Early in one Philadelphia show she slipped and dislocated a neck vertebra, but sang and danced on in agony; unwell on a British tour she collapsed exhausted behind a Manchester theatre curtain as it closed, and in Mexico continued seemingly unperturbed during an earthquake.

When the pop hits died in 1969 – and there'd been exactly fifty in the States – she returned to Country from which she'd come, no longer the anachronism with the off-stage lollipop.

15

Neil Sedaka

Neil Sedaka was still at Brooklyn's Lincoln High School when a number he'd composed with lyricist classmate Howard Greenfield for the Shepherd Sisters, *Stupid Cupid*, instead became a smash for Connie Francis in 1958 (US: No. 14; UK: No. 1). Fame and fortune beckoned.

This pop output was one half of Neil's musical Jekyll and Hyde persona – the other involved excelling at classical piano – adopted originally to avoid being a social outcast at teenage parties. Once there he offered Chopin/Sedaka cocktails to general applause.

During the late Fifties/early Sixties Sedaka and Greenfield's fruitful partnership yielded over 500 opuses, several of which resulted in the slightly chubby Neil finding unlikely pop idol status after RCA snapped him up as an artist. Once Britannia rules the airwaves, though, our tennis fan returned to writing.

Fuelled by British demand, in the Seventies Sedaka made a recording and performing comeback, his canvases broader than ever, the talent honed to a new perfection.

Alexis Korner's Blues Incorporated

Denied the opportunity to perform the music they favoured in public, Parisian-born Alexis Korner (guitar, vocals) and rotund singing harmonica-blower Cyril 'Squirrel' Davies – pictured at the microphone – simply organized their own club. Their rhythm and blues haven opened on St Patrick's Day, 17 March 1962, beneath the picturesquely named ABC Tea Shop, Ealing, West London.

A fabulous nursery attracting soon-to-become-major-names like Rolling Stones Mick Jagger, Keith Richard(s) and Brian Jones, seemingly everyone sat in with the owners' resident outfit, Blues Incorporated, which apart from Korner and Davies was a fluid body of men including drummer Charlie Watts.

Jack Good, that pioneer of British rock 'n' roll television, persuaded a reluctant Decca to allow him to record an Inc. set during one of their alternative Thursday evening West End club gigs, but so certain were the A&R Department that blues would never 'take off' here they issued Jack's baby, *R&B From The Marquee* (November), at budget price; then watched dumbstruck as it sold thousands. It still does.

Del Shannon

The name Del was adopted from his favourite motor, the Cadillac De Ville; Shannon was borrowed from a wrestler who regularly visited the Michigan night spot in which he played guitar. Well, it sounded better as a stage name than Charles Westover.

A radio operator with the US 7th Army stationed in Stuttgart, Germany, as the Sixties began, a lucky break in a Forces show had convinced him to stick with music after demobilization. The singing happened by chance: Shannon was pushed into it when a resident crooner was too inebriated to stand.

New York's Big Top label offered a recording outlet which proved immediately lucrative: Del, unusually, scripted his own hard-edged teen-angst vignettes and *Runaway*, with its frantic Musitron-organ scream plus the ex-GI's major-to-minor key changes and swooping falsetto, sold a rapid million and launched a series.

Regularly in the UK, he introduced the Beatles' music to America by covering their *From Me To You* six months before the 'Fabs' made waves Stateside themselves, but tragically took his own life in 1990.

Sam Cooke

A Chicago baptist minister's son who joined the biggest gospel group in America, the Soul Stirrers, for almost six years before becoming one of the most influential black R&B/pop artists ever, Sam Cooke's premature and controversial death from gunshot wounds at a motel in 1964 robbed popular music of an awesome talent.

Unlike most stars of the period, black or white, Cooke was an entrepreneur, and after selling 1.7 million copies of his *You Send Me* disc in 1957 set up two publishing companies and a record label, Sar/Derby, to discover and promote other acts. Johnnie Taylor, Lou Rawls, Billy Preston and Bobby Womack all entered the showbiz mainstream courtesy of Cooke, who pacted himself to mighty RCA in January 1960.

An innovative songwriter, *Wonderful World*, *Shake*, *Chain Gang* and *Bring It On Home To Me* were amongst Sam's creations, and his prediction of a black uprising in *A Change Is Gonna Come* showed admirable foresight.

Cooke's funeral produced scenes of mass hysteria.

Jess Conrad

Back in 1957 teenager Gerald James was a flower-vendor near Marble Arch, a stone's throw from London's showbiz heart. Each morning a theatrical agent purchased a buttonhole from him, one day remarking to an acquaintance of the youngster, 'He sells flowers like a born actor and ought to be on the stage.'

Gerry agreed, talked his way into repertory and mastered the craft but, owing to the existence of a like-named Shakespearean actor, adopted the billing Jess Conrad.

Experience brought versatility: major television, cinema, theatre roles all beckoned, and still do, though back in 1960 Decca additionally visualized a pop star. Two minor notations, *Cherry Pie* and *Pretty Jenny*, sandwiched the more substantial *Mystery Girl* (No. 18, 1961), then nothing until 1975 saw one of his 'miss' 45s from that former term, *This Pullover/Why Am I Living*, suddenly elevated to dubious prominence thanks to zany British radio dj Kenny Everett's 'All-Time Worst Records' entertainment. BOTH sides picked up votes, and Jess was delighted!

Eden Kane

When, on 8 May 1976, Robin Sarstedt waltzed into the British charts with his rendering of Hoagy Carmichael's chestnut, *My Resistance Is Low*, a remarkable treble occurred: seven years previously brother Peter had reached No. 1 with his Sophia Loren-storyline disc, *Where Do You Go To My Lovely*, and eight years earlier still Eden Kane had started the ball rolling with *Well I Ask You* (No. 1). Eden Kane? Correct, although the 1942 Delhi, India-born son of a tea planter's accountant was christened Richard Graham Sarstedt.

The trio had actually cut one 45, *Walking In The Sand*, for Decca in 1966, calling themselves the Brothers Kane, trading on the senior partner's past triumphs – four Top Tenners for Edward Lewis's baby over 1961 to 1962 and a finale, *Boys Cry* (No. 8, 1964) elsewhere – before the cabaret circuit employed immaculately attired Eden, once nicknamed 'the Beau Brummell of Popsters'; his original break had been in May 1960 via confectioner Cadbury's sponsored talent contest, though the initial resulting disc for Pye, aptly called *Hot Chocolate Crazy*, didn't 'stir' imaginations.

Jet Harris

The airstream sobriquet bestowed upon Terence Harris was a reference to his having been a sprint champion at school, but this great, great nephew of revered music hall entertainer Vesta Tilley caused quite a showbiz sensation in Britain in 1962 when, just after collecting an umpteenth award with his three Shadows' colleagues and Cliff Richard on 15 April, he announced his departure for solo status. Twelve days later the ace musician had signed with Decca and linked up with another former 'silhouette', drummer-turned-house producer, Tony Meehan.

Thus began a new chapter for the Fender Bass VI practitioner who achieved a unique sound by tuning down an octave; he experienced brief disc triumph with instrumental bankers *Diamonds* (UK: No. 1), *Scarlett O'Hara* (No. 2) and *Applejack* (No. 4) – on which Meehan shared billing after performing, uncredited, on two singles anonymously. His success was marred by personal despair, which brought likeable Jet's front-line career to a premature end.

Chris Montez

Christopher Montanez attended the same California seat of learning as the Beach Boys, which wasn't a bad start. His brothers provided guitar tuition, and at fifteen he began singing and writing songs using neighbourhood chicano rocker Ritchie Valens (*Donna; La Bamba*) as his role model.

A good idea as it turned out: talent-seeking writer/producer Jim Lee conceived a new record label around him and, now as Chris Montez, he notched a localized hit first time out with his own *All You Had To Do Was Tell Me*. The January 1943-born hopeful's mentor crafted the second though, and *Let's Dance* sold a global million in 1962, as did its sequel which the pair co-wrote, *Some Kinda Fun*. Decca's London-American offshoot had wisely picked up both.

Montez toured Britain, headlining above the Beatles, just after his twentieth birthday, later exercising that laid-back, amiable nasal monotone on hits for A&M like *Call Me* and *The More I See You*.

23

Billy Fury

Billy Fury, Decca's original Liverpool star, provided them with more United Kingdom singles chart notations – 26 between February 1959 and August 1966 – than any other artist. He was cruelly denied a No. 1, settling instead for a penultimate slot thanks to 1961's *Jealousy* and a trio of No. 3s: *Halfway To Paradise*, his biggest seller overall, from that same year, and the consecutive 1963 outings *Like I've Never Been Gone* and *When Will You Say I Love You.*

Fury was initially an unbridled rock 'n' roller who created Britain's finest authentic effort in this direction with a ten-inch album entitled *The Sound Of Fury* (1960). On it Joe Brown picked guitar and 'Scouse' vocal group, the Four Jays – later, toting instruments, re-christened the Fourmost – were flown to London at Fury's expense to participate, but Decca viewed Ronald Wycherley – Bill's real name – as a beat-balladeer, discouraged his songwriting and tamed his stage act. He thrived throughout the Mersey boom without ever emphasizing his roots, but ill-health and psychedelia conspired to nudge him sideways thereafter, a promising 'comeback' ended by fatal heart failure on 28 January 1983.

Heinz

As bass player of the Tornados Heinz Burt collected the first ever International Gold Award given by Uncle Sam's *Cash Box* magazine to recognize their achievement with the 1962 global five million seller, *Telstar*, written by the disc's producer, Joe Meek.

In April 1963 the German-born blond six-footer quit for a solo shot though, jettisoned his surname and on 4 May, still under Meek's guidance, launched himself as a Decca vocalist on both vinyl and TV at home.

The single, *Dreams Do Come True*, was a wistful ballad totally at odds with Heinz's stage act and failed, but Meek's right-hand-man, Geoff Goddard, came up with a more appropriate opus paying homage to the late Mr Cochran, *Just Like Eddie*, and it romped to No. 5.

Four lesser placings and a label switch followed before he slipped from sight, although a young Ritchie Blackmore wielded some mean guitar circa 1964 in his backing crew, the Wild Boys.

Peter, Paul & Mary

Judy Garland reckoned they had 'Pow', 'they' being folk trio Peter (Yarrow – pictured right), Paul (Stookey) and Mary (Allin Travers), an early-Sixties American sensation, initially on the college campus circuit, who introduced some of Bob Dylan's earliest outpourings to a wider audience than might otherwise have been reached.

Coming together in New York during 1961 and signed to the newly incorporated Warner Brothers Records, their first three albums spent a combined total of 364 weeks on Uncle Sam's Top 200, but horrified by the overbearing commercial acceptance attained, during a nationwide British broadcast from the London Palladium they perplexed promotion men by *not* plugging their latest single.

The worldwide protest movement's favourites split in 1971, reforming, less successfully, seven years later, during which hiatus Yarrow had co-written and produced Mary MacGregor's international blockbuster *Torn Between Two Lovers* (1976), leaving 5 feet $9\frac{1}{2}$ inch-tall Kentucky native Mary to discover that one of her Gold-plated P, P & M albums held within its grooves the voice of ... Dean Martin.

The Cavern Club, Liverpool

If, in January 1962, anyone had said that barely a year from that date the powers that controlled 'pop' music in Britain would forsake London for a new Mecca, some tatty little cellar at 10 Mathew Street, Liverpool, formerly a storage area for imported Irish bacon, but since the late Fifties a live music venue called the Cavern, they would probably have been certified immediately. That, however, is exactly what happened.

Once the Beatles charted with *Love Me Do*, representatives of all four of the existing British major record companies descended like flies, pens cocked. The Cavern, naturally, wasn't alone, myriad other clubs like the Iron Door, Blue Angel and Jacaranda too supported the north-western seaport's incredibly active – and diverse – music scene, but that 750-capacity unlicensed, much-loved hole-in-the-ground was regarded as the hub.

Among the acts captured by Decca during their talent raids in and around that hotbed locality were the Big Three, the Mojos, Freddie Starr and the Midnighters, the Dennisons, Beryl Marsden, the Young Ones, the Orchids and Lee Curtis and the All Stars.

1964

The Ronettes

1961: teenage sisters Veronica 'Ronnie' and Estelle Bennett (centre and right respectively), along with their younger cousin Nedra Talley, New Yorkers all, were singing and dancing together at the 'City-They-Named-Twice's' famed Peppermint Lounge, having started out while still at high school in 1959.

A single with Colpix Records, billed as Ronnie and the Relatives, did little, a fate awaiting their subsequent Ronettes discs for the label, but once flamboyant artist/producer Phil Spector signed them to his own Philles organization and then invested four months of effort in and lavished his *Be My Baby* (US: No. 2; UK: No. 4) on the trio, a global million-seller quickly ensued.

In January 1964 they toured Britain with the Rolling Stones, record-wise thereafter collecting lesser placings with equally ambitious instrumentations such as *Baby I Love You* (US: No. 24; UK: No. 11) and *Walking In The Rain* (US: No. 23), until Estelle and Nedra opted, in 1966, for family lives; lead vocalist Ronnie married Spector in 1968. They divorced six years later, though she still sporadically offers new inspirations.

The Rockin' Berries

The Rockin' Berries – or at least a collection of individuals still sporting that title – have outlasted many of their 1960s rivals by pursuing a policy of family entertainment, with particular emphasis on comedy and impersonations, but the original combo were, as their name implied, worshippers at the shrines of Chuck Berry, Little Richard and Elvis.

Inhabitants of Birmingham, they toiled in smoky German clubs over much of 1962 and early 1963. Once back in Britain Clive Lea (vocals), Geoff Turton and Chuck Botfield (guitars), Roy Austin (bass) and Terry Bond (drums) expunged their twin-saxophone augmentation and flying quintet colours; they were signed by Decca where two singles, the group-penned *Wah Wah Wah Woo* followed by a blast at James Ray's 1962 US profiler, *Itty Bitty Pieces*, surfaced to minimal appreciation.

A move to Pye's Piccadilly division yielded six hits from 1964 to 1966, including Top Tenners *He's In Town* and *Poor Man's Son*; later, in 1969, a disguised Turton, solo as 'Jefferson', hit paydirt in the US.

George Harrison and Phil Spector

The outfits – close-fitting mohair suits, frilly dress shirts, multi-coloured silk cloaks and dark glasses – were as outlandish as his unsurpassed production techniques. Young Phil Spector, who in 1958 had written/performed, as one-third of the Teddy Bears, an enchanting little seven-figure retailing ballad stickered *To Know Him Is To Love Him*, six years later was utilizing seemingly every bookable musician to create, as he put it, 'a Wagnerian approach to rock 'n' roll; little symphonies for the kids'.

That and more he achieved via his Philles set up which, over 1961 to 1966, notched up hit after hit from, particularly, the Righteous Brothers, Ronettes, Crystals, Darlene Love and Ike and Tina Turner.

When Americans basically passed on the latter couple's *River Deep – Mountain High* – it collapsed at No. 88 – a wounded Spector left music for two years, feeling his masterpiece had been shunned.

The chap on the left did OK as well. George Harrison strummed guitar with a quartet from Liverpool named after humble insects, though their spelling was eccentric . . . .

Ben E. King

Having fronted the 'new' Drifters – a fivesome formerly called the Crowns who assumed their better-known guise in 1959 at the behest of one George Treadwell, owner of the name – Ben E. King then sang lead on gems like *There Goes My Baby* and *Save The Last Dance For Me.*

In May 1960 Benjamin Earl Nelson – for it was he – took flight alone, signed to Atco in the US and in just three hours taped four numbers which would keep him in milk and cookies ad infinitum, among them *Spanish Harlem*, a Jerry Leiber collaboration with his 'apprentice', one Phil Spector, and *Stand By Me* which Henderson, North Carolina's finest, had a hand in writing himself.

As the 'swinging' decade moved forward, King's prominence waned until 1975's *Supernatural Thing*, and thereafter duet duties with the Average White Band restored good fortune, following which Ben again courted cabaret patrons. 1986–7 though brought a welcome double reprise for *Stand*: in a Stephen King movie and as underpinning for a jeans' television commercial. Re-cue smiles . . . .

Jack Jackson

Pete Murray

Alan Freeman

Jimmy Savile

Disc Jockeys

Before, first, Radio Caroline, officially from Easter Sunday, 29 March 1964, and then a host of other offshore commercial 'pirate' stations, began beaming their diet of non-stop Top 40 pop music programmes at the youth of Britain and mainland Europe, the UK was poorly served. Only a tiny handful of BBC shows and, at night, the blessing of the London-taped output of Radio Luxembourg offered succour, even if the 208 radio signal did fade and boom on its medium wave atmospheric-troubled roller coaster.

Major disc jockeys of the period were Jack Jackson with his *Juke Box* and *Record Round-Up* and Pete Murray's *Top Pops* and *Record Show*, while Jimmy Savile handled the Warner Brothers and Decca-sponsored *Teen & Twenty Disc Club* spectacles, Australian Alan 'Fluff' Freeman weighing in with an actual Decca label showcase from November 1962 until fronting the Beeb's all-important *Pick Of The Pops* on Sunday afternoons.

Both Savile and Freeman were Decca recording artists also, the latter's *Madison Time* – released to coincide with his Luxembourg opening – retailing the least number of copies of any disc to that date ever issued by a UK major, just seventeen! Thirty years on, both spinners are still at the top of their chosen profession.

The Crystals

Phil Spector was walking through the corridor of a Broadway music publisher's building in May 1961 when he heard five girls rehearsing their vocals in an office. So taken was the Bronx-born, ex-Fairfax Junior High, Hollywood, pupil with the sweetness which greeted his ears, he strode straight into the room and politely demanded to know what its occupants were doing that evening. Fortunately, nothing in particular; Phil signed and recorded them before midnight struck. Hey presto, Philles's first act materialized.

Mary Thomas, and then Pat Wright, withdrew to take husbands rather than the tour bus, leaving (left to right) Barbara Alston, Dolores 'LaLa' Brooks, Frances Collins – Wright's replacement in 1963 – and Dee Dee Kennibrew.

The initial group grew out of a fun singalong at a party, took their billing from songwriter Leroy Bates' daughter, Crystal, and stormed worldwide ratings with *Da Doo Ron Ron*, *Then He Kissed Me* and *He's A Rebel*, to mention but three, although Darlene Love and the Blossoms actually performed the last cited.

Peter Jay & The Jaywalkers

All action, that was the law by which drummer/vibist Peter Jay & the Jaywalkers lived, both off-stage and on.

Originally a raucous seven-piece purely instrumental outfit completed by Peter 'Buzz' Miller (lead guitar), Tony 'Napoleon' Webster (rhythm), Johnny 'Snowy' Larke (bass, 2nd lead), 'Lolly' Lloyd Baker (piano, baritone sax), Jeff 'Seaweed' Moss (acoustic bass) and Mac 'Toots' McIntyre (tenor sax, flute), they attracted Decca who put them under contract just before the Beatles' *Love Me Do* was issued.

Coming off the starting blocks was a dynamite sax-led oldie adaptation, *Can Can '62*, which, though it only danced to No. 31, definitely loitered and pre-dated Bad Manners' similar irreverence by almost two decades.

Autumn 1963 saw them actually warming up audiences on John, Paul, George and Ringo's cross-country pilgrimage but, even after adding a vocalist in the person of fifteen-year-old Terry Reid (yes, *that* one), fame remained elusive so Jay, whose hobby was action-painting, scattered his much replaced disciples in 1966.

Kathy Kirby

Lots of girls dream of singing with a large, well-known orchestra. Kathy Kirby did it, simply by walking up to the elevated bandstand upon which the tuxedo-clad leader stood and tugging at his trouser leg until he paid attention.

The little blonde with the big voice belted out a couple of 'standards' there and then, to wild applause, and Bert Ambrose, maestro of Britain's top dance band of the 1930s and 1940s who, twenty years on, was in the twilight of his behind-the-footlights activities, put her on the payroll, later adopting a management function.

Added subsequently to the cast of a weekly fifteen million plus viewer TV variety show, Kathy, the lip-glossed, poodle-loving 'Golden Girl' – her companion was called Bobo before you ask – became best-known for a 1963 revival of Sammy Fain and Paul Francis Webster's 1953 'Best Song' Oscar-winner, *Secret Love*, until personal tragedies marred the Seventies for her.

Albeit with a lower profile, happily today the vivacious operatically trained East Londoner has bounced back.

The Applejacks

In 1964 it was impossible to open the local broadsheet which advised the residents of the Midlands town of Solihull, Warwickshire, about Women's Institute meetings or 'seedy' goings-on at the Horticultural Society, without also encountering the smiling faces of neighbourhood pop celebrities, the Applejacks.

Left to right Martin Baggott (lead guitar), Phil Cash (rhythm), bespectacled Gerry Freeman (drums), Al Jackson (vocals), Megan Davies (bass) and Don Gould (keyboards); they'd developed from a 1961 skiffle three-piece, the Crestas, into pop instrumental quintet the Jaguars – obviously auto fixationists – until finally picking on Applejacks as a derivation of their newly recruited singer's name.

Attracting regular over-capacity houses at the Civic Centre, Decca swooped via a three-year deal, put them in their studios for five and a half hours, and then watched the result, *Tell Me When*, skate to No. 7.

Beatles John and Paul donated a follow-up, *Like Dreamers Do* (No. 20), when both outfits met at a TV rehearsal, but after one further placing they returned to gigging from whence they came.

Roy Orbison

It was almost a portent of things to come that Roy Orbison preferred to be clad in head-to-toe black, including the trademark glasses, and thrived on emotion-packed 'loser' numbers, for while he enjoyed huge success as a singer/songwriter his personal life was fraught with family deaths which would have destroyed lesser men.

One of the celebrity late-Fifties graduates from Sam Phillips' Memphis Sun nursery, he moved to Monument Records where hits like *Only The Lonely*, *Running Scared* and *It's Over* made him an international sensation.

For London-American, who licensed the label outside the States, he was their most successful artist ever; and when he transferred allegiance in the US to MGM in July 1965, he insisted Decca's offshoot retain twenty-year issue rights elsewhere for his future output. Roy sold more discs in Britain during 1964 than any other American.

Hit singles ceased with the arrival of the Seventies, then a huge Eighties renaissance was cruelly terminated by his death from a heart attack on 6 December 1988. RIP, 'Big O'.

Dave Berry

One of the Sixties' most adventurous artistes, David Holgate Grundy – Dave Berry to you and I, the pseudonym borrowed from his idol, R&B star Chuck – was a son of Sheffield who modelled his vocal style on Snooks Eaglin and Slim Harpo, took accompaniment from the Cruisers and employed a full-time lighting operative on tour to illuminate his abstract stage movements.

Producer Mickie Most brought Dave and friends to Albert Embankment but passed them to resident A&R man Mike Smith almost immediately. When the players next took an unheard of eight hours to perfect one track, *Memphis, Tennessee*, disbelieving Decca bosses decreed thereafter session men be booked. Enter guitarists Big Jim Sullivan and Jimmy Page with bassist John Paul Jones.

Our rock-theatre pioneer with the upturned collar secured eight hits here between 1963 and 1966 – including three No. 5s – but found greater acclaim across Europe, particularly Holland, where his interpretation of Kink Ray Davies's *This Strange Effect* became the country's biggest-ever selling single (1965).

The Big Three

Had fate not decreed otherwise, the Big Three surely would, as they should, have fulfilled in a commercial sense the adjective their billing proclaimed. In every other respect they did.

Evolving out of a late-Fifties Liverpool combo, Cass and the Casanovas, the classic line-up boasted Johnny Hutchinson (drums, vocals), Brian Griffiths (lead guitar) and Johnny Gustafson – later a Merseybeat – (bass). Our 'collectors' illustration reveals a post-November 1963 incarnation with 'Hutch' left-flanked by another Scouse legend, Bill Russley, aka Faron – 'The Panda-Footed Prince Of Prance' – once of Faron's Flamingos fame.

The 'original' participants – a revolutionary hard rockin' 'Power Trio' – had Brian Epstein management, the respect/idolization of almost every other muso for miles around, and live were *the* loudest act: Hutchinson 'modified' his drums; reversed the sticks, and his axemen used custom-made amplifiers, nicknamed 'coffins'; unfortunately Decca needed them back overnight from a Hamburg gig for a recording debut which did them scant justice, exhausted as they were. Two minor hits, personnel changes and ultimate dissipation sold them *very* short.

Carl Perkins

Brought to Britain in May 1964 by Brunswick to co-headline a nationwide trek with Chuck Berry, supported by the Animals and British Decca's Nashville Teens, US Decca's new signing Carl Perkins stopped off at West Hampstead to preserve a handful of numbers on magnetic oxide for them and was so taken with the reaction he received both on and off stage he publicly discussed the possibility of settling here with his family. It came to nothing.

Four of his greatest fans were the Beatles who not only took the opportunity to jam with the man who'd warned everybody not to step on his *Blue Suede Shoes* back in 1956, but soon afterwards paid him the sincerest compliment by recording three Perkins copyrights, namely *Matchbox*, *Honey Don't* and *Everybody's Trying To Be My Baby*.

Since then he has variously accompanied old pal Johnny Cash on the road, scored films and flown flags for both country and rock 'n' roll.

Davie Jones & The King Bees

Like Marc Bolan, another latter-day musical icon/fashion chameleon who began at Decca in the 1960s but didn't triumph until the decade changed, David Bowie threaded his way through a few costume – and name – amendments long before any Spiders descended from Mars. In the beginning there was Davie Jones and the King Bees.

DJ had been encouraged to follow an obvious melodic leaning by his art instructor, who also suggested a liaison with his own similarly 'afflicted' son, one Peter Frampton. Point taken, and twenty-five years later . . . though that's another story.

David learned saxophone; gigged with a couple of groups; formed the Hive-dwellers and thence acquired a manager and one-off deal with Decca subsidiary, Vocalion. Their single, *Liza Jane* was voted a hit by television's *Juke Box Jury* panel, wasn't, and the act split up. David's latest guise would return to Albert Embankment in 1966.

Trivia buffs note: in 1964 a library typist erroneously added the KB's titles to another new Jones's filing card, Tom's!

The Pete Best Four

If they'd let the Beatles slip through their fingers owing to an A&R policy dictate, then at least when one ex-member was up for grabs the London-based major moved in swiftly when Pete Best formed his quartet in the autumn of 1963 with bassist Wayne Bickerton, lead guitarist Tony Waddington and Tommy McGuirh on rhythm.

Cutting demo tapes, Pete's mother then acted as their manageress. Mike Smith, who'd wanted to sign him with three other guys the first time, stepped in and on 21 February they cut two titles, *Fortune Teller/Why Did I Fall In Love With You*, followed on 22 April by *You've Got Everything*, *I'm Gonna Knock On Your Door* and *A Shot Of Rhythm And Blues*. *Door/Why* appeared as a solitary single on 19 June but was bypassed by Joe Public.

Pete drifted into oblivion but Messrs Bickerton and Waddington later became producers/songwriters and label managers for Deram, enjoying considerable success in the Seventies with their own State Records.

P. J. Proby

'Following the outstanding success of his single *Hold Me*, Decca are to release early this month an EP by the same artist to be headlined simply *P. J. Proby*. One of the most talked-about stars on today's disc scene, P. J. sings four exciting tracks in his own personal style . . . .' So read an internal Decca press release in October 1964.

Unfortunately, most of the 'talking' within months would refer to good ol' Texas boy James Marcus Smith's habit of splitting his velvet breeches on stage. The EP was cancelled, but only because the one-time Jett Powers was apparently still under contract to America's Liberty Records who, seeing their previously obscure act riding consecutive Top Tenners in Britain – *Together* was the other – issued a court order preventing Decca from capitalizing further on the new star Jack Good visualized, brought to England and recorded. He was thus lost to both through a probably innocent oversight by all concerned.

Ironically, 'Big Jim's' expulsion from a February 1965 Cilla Black tour here created a vacancy . . . for Tom Jones.

43

The Fairies

Originally Dane Stevens and the Deep Beats, this band, hailing from the historic garrison town of Colchester, Essex, adopted the Fairies name in 1964.

A well-supported collection of R&B fanatics who cited Howlin' Wolf, Muddy Waters and Jimmy Reed as having influenced them, oddly their five taped excursions produced covers of Fats Waller's *Honeysuckle Rose*, Gene Vincent's *Be-Bop-A-Lula*, Glenn Miller – and later Fats Domino's – *Blueberry Hill* – all unissued – while for their solitary (unsuccessful) single, a run at Dylan's *Don't Think Twice, It's Alright* emerged.

Comprising Stevens (piano, drums, harmonica, vocals), Michael 'Mick' Weaver (lead guitar, keyboards) and Johns Gandy (bass), Acutt (rhythm) and Alder (drums), they made a good noise live and with their free-form 'Fairy Dance' had caught both the ears and eyes of Decca's Richard Lloyd. Cheap to keep, when touring they slept in a tent out of preference, before disbanding (frozen?) in 1965.

As 'Twink' Alder has subsequently carved a colourful career, while Weaver's name has garnished many album sleeves. His stated ambition? to grow bananas . . . .

Zoot Money & His Big Roll Band

Heirs apparent to Georgie Fame's residency at London's noted Flamingo Club in 1964, George Bruno – aka Zoot Money – (keyboards, vocals), Neville Newall (tenor sax), Clive Burrows (baritone sax), Andy Somers (guitar), Paul Williams (bass) and Colin Allen (drums) cut four sides for Decca that spring, later moving to EMI's Columbia imprint which did not particularly improve their fortunes, although live they were big news.

Zoot – after his jazz sax hero Mr Sims – was an extrovert of the first order, and with the psychedelic onslaught apparent he and Andy (Summers) – later of the Police – folded the Big Roll and adopted kaftans to ride their Dantalion's Chariot, later still becoming two of Eric Burdon's New Animals. Money, who loved elaborate costumes anyway, donned another for his gig as best man at Eric's wedding too.

George repressed his natural front-man tendencies to back numerous others down subsequent years, while Williams courted Juicy Lucy and Allen percussed with Focus.

The Rolling Stones

Absolute catalysts in the overall development of the 'Swinging Sixties' as dictated to the world by Great Britain, the Rolling Stones were also the recording jewel in Decca's crown, pacted after the organization's talent scouts went on a beat-group signing spree in the wake of missing out on the Beatles.

Messrs. Jagger, Richard(s), Jones, Wyman, Watts and pianist Ian Stewart gravitated by various means to Alexis Korner's blues hangout in Ealing. The band was founded in 1962 and named after a Muddy Waters song. The Stones acquired a residency at the Crawdaddy Club, Richmond, Surrey. They pulled a crowd with their wild music, signed management forms with nineteen-year-old ex-Beatles public relations man turned ambitious entrepreneur Andrew Loog Oldham (and his partner, Eric Easton) and lured Decca A&R operatives to see them in May 1963. The rest was a cleverly engineered foregone conclusion.

Oldham's brilliant 'rebellious' image moulding for his charges – from the outset he moved the 'straight-looking' Stewart behind the scenes – coupled with the band's infectious sounds, many soon self-conceived, and their snook-cocking at authority had them storming global best-sellers. An amended line-up still does.

Mick Jagger

Although Brian Jones was initially considered leader of the group, their charismatic vocalist, harmonica-blower and maracas-rattler, Michael Philip Jagger from Dartford in the hop-picking county of Kent since 26 July 1943, was the one who caught the eye with his animated on-stage antics, and gave particularly good copy to journalists off it, being far more outgoing than the shy Jones and exceeding his high-profile controversy quotient.

Co-writer, with Keith Richard(s), of most original band repertoire, the cricket-loving Jagger's generous lips wrapped themselves around an impressive tally of hits, from the June 1963-issued cover of a lesser-known Chuck Berry rave, *Come On* (UK: No. 21), the Rollers rush-released debut on black plastic, through timeless own-initiates such as the transatlantic roof-toppers *(I Can't Get No) Satisfaction* (1965), *Paint It Black* (1966) and *Honky Tonk Women* (1969), their final 45 for Albert Embankment and its sisters before opening their own eponymous label with distribution elsewhere.

Mick has also tried his hand at acting via *Ned Kelly* and *Performance*, both big-screeners from 1970.

Bill Wyman

Charlie Watts

Bill Wyman and Charlie Watts

It may be all action, limbs a-flailing at the front of the stage whenever the Rolling Stones are in concert, but in direct contrast the group's 'senior citizen' rhythm section, Lewisham, London-born William Perks – alias Bill Wyman – and from the capital's Islington district, Charlie Watts, have always remained relatively motionless at the back of the stand.

In the early days Wyman's 'gimmick' was to cuddle his Framus bass in an upright position – which was probably quite restrictive – but now its various replacements tend to hang rather more in the standard horizontal mode. Always the unit's self-appointed archivist, in recent years he has spread his wings by opening a London restaurant decorated with Stones' memorabilia called, aptly, *Sticky Fingers*, after their first post-Decca album of 1971, and provided a valuable insight into the colourful history of the 'Greatest Rock 'n' Roll Band In The World' via his biographical book, *Stone Alone*.

Jazz fanatic C. Watts though had long beaten him into print, having published his tribute to alto-saxophonist Charlie Parker, *Ode To A High Flying Bird* back in December 1964, while today maintaining a part-time jazz ensemble to satiate his alternative passion.

Brian Jones and Keith Richards

The Stones' twin six-string department, Brian Jones' (left) neat, sure-fingered lead picking perfectly complemented Keith Richards' – he dropped the 's' for years, only reinstating it in the mid-Seventies – open-stringed rhythm, and both men collected a formidable array of machines upon which to practise their art.

Cheltenham, Gloucestershire, native Jones was actually a highly proficient multi-instrumentalist who stamped his hallmark on the group's early records also through contributions on slide and twelve-string guitars, dulcimer, harpsichord and, notably, sitar, but in June 1969, following drug-related hospitalization, the sensitive young man who had never seemed comfortable in the hard glare of publicity left the outfit and a few weeks later was found dead in the swimming pool at his home. John Mayall Bluesbreaker, Mick Taylor, stepped into the vacancy.

Richards retains his key role today – he's the band's 'heart' – now with Ronnie Wood, an axeman of similar style to his own, sharing duties, although Keith went on the road with other musicians to promote his solo album, *Talk Is Cheap*, in 1988.

The Graham Bond Organization

One of the most abiding memories of the Sixties' club scene was viewing the remarkable Graham Bond simultaneously blowing alto sax and fingering the keyboard of his Hammond organ. When not playing the sax he was a great R&B vocalizer.

Earlier in the decade he'd been one of British jazz's brightest hopes through sax work with Don Rendell's outfit, next joining Blues Incorporated during November 1962. An ongoing fixation with ivoried instruments, though, led to the formation of his own band in February the following year, which was made possible by recruiting singer/bassist/harmonica-doubler Jack Bruce and drummer Ginger Baker, also from Blues Inc.

John McLaughlin's guitar augmented their sound for six months, before tenor player Dick Heckstall-Smith instead fleshed out the foursome which Decca signed, recording them initially on 5 May 1964. Overall nine titles were cut.

Fate unkindly showed them little record success, but after splitting up in 1966 Bruce and Baker would soon taste Cream with Clapton. Tragically Graham died in May 1974.

Elkie Brooks

Salford's Elkie Brooks – née Elaine Bookbinder – began singing at four but on leaving school had to combine such semi-professional exploits with daytime work in her father's confectionery business.

Dubbed 'Manchester's Answer To Brenda Lee', at sixteen she shared airtime with four little-known Beatles on radio's *Talent Spot* who, when they'd made the grade two years on, invited Elkie to join their 1964 Christmas show. By then she'd moved to London, shared stages with such as the Animals, acquired a manager/music director in ex-Shadow Ian Samwell and issued two of her three 45s quota at Decca.

Despite such hopeful activity this sister of Billy J. Kramer's drummer in the Dakotas, Tony Mansfield, failed to click with her cover of Etta James's *Something's Got A Hold On Me*, its follow-up, *Nothing Left To Do But Cry*, or finally the Miracles' *The Way You Do The Things You Do* (1965), little realizing yet another dozen years' patience would be necessary.

Joe Cocker

It was one of life's sweet ironies that gentle Joe Cocker finally made his significant breakthrough in 1968 with a cover of the Beatles' *With A Little Help From My Friends*, for his vinyl debut four summers earlier emanated from that source and *I'll Cry Instead* bombed spectacularly.

A daytime fitter with the East Midlands Gas Board, Joe sang, as Vance Arnold, with brother Vic's group, the Avengers, at night; Decca's Dick Rowe caught Joe in Manchester, signed him and in June, amazingly for those budget-conscious times, taped a session utilizing a 22-piece orchestra in London which was rejected; so they did it again with the Ivy League adding vocals!

What happened to faith though? The single issued on 4 September, ignored at retail, was never followed up. Joe pounded British tarmac with Manfred Mann; toured France and . . . returned to the gas company which had granted six-months leave of absence, but he doesn't install cookers for them any-more . . .

The Moody Blues

When friends Ray Thomas (flute, saxophone, harmonica – second from right) and Mike Pinder (keyboards, vocals – right) returned from 'the madness and diabolical living conditions' – Ray's words – of the Hamburg–Hannover, German club scene in November 1963, they discovered their Birmingham base crawling with 250 bands all vying for the same vacancies. Solution: form a 'supergroup'. Welcome charismatic bassist Clint Warwick (left), lead vocalist/guitarist Denny Laine (centre) and drummer Graeme Edge.

In May 1964, the billing the MB 5 was adopted in honour of their favourite brewery, Mitchell and Butler, with a view to possible sponsorship. None was forthcoming, so they decided to find alternative meanings for those initials. All were moody; all liked blues. Voilà.

Gigging in London and finding favour with Decca, their second 45, a cover of Bessie Banks' *Go Now!* sold a million, but declining fortune thereafter saw Warwick and Laine quit in 1966, to be replaced by Justin Hayward, John Lodge and a new sound which, to date, has shifted some forty million albums worldwide.

Lulu & The Luvvers

Decca made a point of having their talent scouts comb Scotland, and very fruitful it proved. However, nobody had to take the train north to claim Marie McDonald McLoughlin Lawrie's signature, as a London impresario, Marian Massey, had already fetched the fifteen-year-old and her backing crew down to the 'Smoke'.

With a bluesy rasp which belied her age, when initially agent-spotted, Marie was apparently sporting curlers and a fur beret. Within weeks she'd been re-christened Lulu, donned a snappy turquoise leather two-piece, and Ross Nelson (lead guitar), Jim Dewar (rhythm), Tony Tierney (bass), Alec Bell (guitar, keyboards), Jimmy Smith (saxes) and David Miller (drums) – the original line-up – wore a new label, the Luvvers, too. Their account-opening run at the 1959 Isley Brothers' million-selling *Shout* was to prove a durable classic.

Perhaps never absolutely comfortable with R&B despite owning a voice to carry it off, that single nevertheless launched the attractive redhead on a long showbiz career during which she has graciously epitomized the 'all-round-entertainer'.

Rod Stewart

Ten out of ten for accuracy of prediction: 'It was in January that Rod turned fully professional and with TV appearances and his discovery by our A&R man Ray Horricks, this artist will go far.' Thus spake the oracle that was October 1964's biography despatched with promos of Roderick David Stewart's sole single for Decca, *Good Morning Little Schoolgirl.*

Indeed, this football-crazy then-Mod would fulfil the organization's prophecy although not for some years to come nor, unfortunately for them, beneath a 'Supreme Record Company'-owned logo, but his debut was bright enough, being taped at the end of a Jimmy Powell session. The North Londoner picked guitar himself.

That legendary sense of humour was already active; our interviewer was advised: 'All these blues singers going on about walking down the railroad track. They've never done it in their lives. Nor have I. You've got more to sing the blues about in the Archway Road.'

But what's this in the 'Likes' and 'Dislikes' columns? 'Not Very Fond Of . . . Scotland'. Some mistake, surely???

Brian Poole & The Tremeloes

It was through their sharing the same optician that Dagenham, Essex, butcher's son, the Buddy Holly-aping Brian Poole (centre) and his brothers in melody, the Tremeloes, left to right Ricky West(wood) (lead guitar), Dave Munden (drums) and Alans Howard (bass) and Blakely (rhythm), came to the attention of Decca staffer, Mike Smith.

They already had a weekly slot on one of British radio's then few pop showcases, looked the part, were extremely competent musicians and lived near 'town', but it was unfortunate that on the day of their audition, 1 January 1962, they received the thumbs-up rather than the Beatles, for an unfair stigma was attached to them ever after.

Pity poor Smith; he wanted both but only one roster group vacancy existed so was overruled. Given history and track records to that date, the option taken remains justifiable.

Brian and playmates did well together here – eight hits over 1963 to 1965 including the chart-topping *Do You Love Me* – though after splitting in 1966 the group fared better than their former singer. Still mates, lucrative cabaret openings keep both individually on the boards today.

Twinkle

Eminent writer Ted Willis condemned it as 'dangerous drivel', and even television's *Ready Steady Go!* banned it. On the strength of its success upon this sceptred isle, come 11 April 1965 Uncle Sam refused Twinkle a work permit, causing the pretty blonde singer to opine, 'Oh well, I shall have to stay at home working on my novel about the ups and downs of adolescence.'

What heinous crime had the classically trained seventeen-year-old Lyn Ripley committed? Apparently recording her song about *Terry*, teenage motorbiker, who responded to a lover's tiff by roaring off recklessly into the night. You can guess the rest.

Establishment figures may have pooh-poohed it but offshore pirate radio didn't, and Decca's 30 October 1964 seven-incher hurried to No. 4; its non-controversial successor, *Golden Lights*, halted at No. 21 thus ending her chart career within six months.

Incidentally, she didn't stay at home. Labelmates the Bachelors and Mike Preston booked her on their Australia/New Zealand pilgrimage of autumn 1965.

The Righteous Brothers with Cathy McGowan

Americans the Righteous Brothers, Bobby Hatfield (left) and Bill Medley – see here sandwiching Cathy McGowan, presenter of British Independent Television's unmissable Friday evening pop programme, *Ready Steady Go!* – were the first white male vocal duo produced by Phil Spector.

Although they'd been recording since November 1962 for Moonglow, it was following their second small-screen outing on Uncle Sam's *Shindig* that Spector took interest and ensured the tenor/baritone duo would spread his gospel worldwide, after kicking off their Philles association with 1964's *You've Lost That Lovin' Feelin'*, a transatlantic No. 1. 'The only record I've heard which completely overwhelms me,' was how then Stones' mentor Andrew Oldham described it.

Further breathtaking seven-inchers like revivals of Fifties' hits *Ebb Tide* and *Unchained Melody* followed; the twosome moved to Verve in 1966, and then oversaw themselves on disc until splitting, temporarily, in 1968.

Their classics though resurrect themselves every so often – inclusion on the soundtrack of 1990's box-office-breaking movie, *Ghost*, made *Unchained* the best-selling UK single that term. Quality will out, indefinitely . . .

Crispian St Peters

Inspired by Country gentlemen Hanks Snow and Williams – and girls with long dark hair – Crispian St Peters' salad days came in 1966 after covering Californian pop quintet the We Five's American No. 3 of the previous summer, *You Were On My Mind* (UK: No. 2), eighteen months down the road belatedly selling it to our cousins again (No. 36). *The Pied Piper* (UK: No. 5; US: No. 4) and *Changes* (No. 47; No. 57) wrapped up his intrusions on published 'hot' vinyl tabulations.

Born Robin Peter Smith in Swanley, Kent in 1944, his youth club leader introduced the amateur boxer to guitar playing which led to the formation of his own group, called, unusually, Beat Formula Three. Noticing an advertisement requesting would-be singers contact a newly formed record company for auditions paid immediate dividends: it introduced the aspirant to David Nicolson, who became Cris's manager/producer and sold Decca on their collaborations.

Ten singles, an EP and album found their way into shops between February 1965's *At This Moment* and December 1968's *Carolina*, much of this output being self-penned.

The Zombies

Precociously talented in more ways than one – they had 50 'O' levels between them – the Zombies, left to right Hugh Grundy (drums), Colin Blunstone (vocals), Paul Atkinson (lead guitar), Rod Argent (keyboards) and Chris White (bass), won a beat-group competition sponsored by a major London evening newspaper. This led to greater things.

Inspired by the jazz/classical music-influenced Argent, whose song constructions clearly showed his preferences and called into play time signatures and arrangements few outfits in pop then would have heard of, much less considered using, with Blunstone's distinctive throat emissions, these Hertfordshire-based academics were signed by a music publisher who in turn leased their tapes to Decca.

Clearing a cool million first time out via Rod's ultra-sophisticated *She's Not There* (UK: No. 12; US: No. 2, 1964), they found greater appreciation abroad from then on, Decca seemingly unsure how to sell the polished diamonds delivered.

A move to CBS in 1967 brought positive results only after they'd disbanded, Rod, with his unit Argent, and Blunstone thereafter enjoying the most conspicuous plaudits. All deserved more.

Unit Four plus Two

No less an entertainment industry giant than Miss Gracie Fields always insisted that if a song was 'hit' material, she'd know two thirds of the lyrics after one hearing. Most of us who've ever earned our living by playing records to the masses would add that it needs to make its impact within fifteen seconds. Unit Four plus Two's self-penned *Concrete And Clay* satisfied both criteria.

With its unique cowbell-and-glass intro chased by nimble guitar figures and oblique title/storyline, it shot the six-piece from Hertfordshire to the top on 5 April 1965, consequently deposing labelmates Mick Jagger and Co.'s *The Last Time*.

Originally a vocal quartet, Unit Four, assembled in 1962, poor health caused Brian Parker's relocation to offshore duties, leaving his colleagues Tommy 'Sweat' Moeller (keyboards, guitar, lead vocals), 'Buster' Meikle (guitar) and Peter 'the Count' Moules (vocals) – fourth to second from right respectively – to recruit Rodney Garwood (bass, vocals – right), 'Lem' Lubin (guitar – far left) and Hugh 'Pigmy' Halliday (drums). Enter 'plus Two', and stardom. . . .

The Who

The Who's personnel began to gel back in 1959 when Pete Townshend (guitar – left) and John Entwistle (bass – second from left) formed the Confederates. Three years on vocalist Roger Daltrey (second from right) invited them to throw in their lot with him and drummer Doug Sandon in the Detours.

After months of minor bookings, publicist Pete Meaden convinced the foursome that championing the burgeoning 'Mod' trend would secure their musical future; Sandon departed, and in 1964 Keith Moon (right) appeared.

With one failed single (as the High Numbers) behind them and rejection slips from both EMI and Decca itself, following new management and the support of Anglophile US producer Shel Talmy – handling The Bachelors for the blue and silver label – and a belting Townshend number, *I Can't Explain*, they entered by the back door, signing to American Decca and thus gracing its external equivalent, Brunswick, elsewhere – ironically marketed by Decca GB.

Via this circuitous route these instrument smashers powered to international fame.

Drummers

There are musicians and musicians, but when it comes to pure physical effort and/or a need to vent one's frustrations in a melodic manner, then hammering on a drum kit is, without doubt, the most satisfying form of self-expression.

Few trap-rattlers have ever caught the eye and imagination, nor been such personalities, as the Who's Keith Moon who, unlike most of his contemporaries, was never content to hide behind a battery of snares, basses, tom-toms and cymbals. Oh no, once he'd finished skilfully beating hell out of them on a gig, the Wembley, Middlesex-born extrovert often blew them up. A fine player, his entire existence was prone to wild excesses only terminated by tragic death in 1978 from an overdose of a drug prescribed to combat alcoholism.

Tom Jones, on the other hand, has long been noted for letting his powerful vocal chords make the statements, although it's a little-known fact that Wales' favourite son started out as a self-taught drummer in the valleys, for some time exercising a definite talent in the De Avalons while perfecting his rhythmic sense.

Keith Moon

Tom Jones

Tom Jones & The Playboys

One of Decca's greatest assets and Britain's most popular, consistent exports, Tom Jones (right) – here with his backing group the Playboys, who evolved into the Squires – sold the equivalent of 100 million singles for the company internationally between January 1965's *It's Not Unusual* (UK: No. 1; US: No. 10), and a fatefully titled blue and silver farewell a decade later, September 1975's *Memories Don't Leave Like People Do*. Almost thirty years on his catalogue remains a prized possession, both artistically and financially.

Initially Tommy Scott, an experienced rock 'n' roller of eight years standing, he was spotted in concert by fellow Welshman Gordon Mills, once a harmonica champion but by 1964 songwriting and seeking a client to manage. Their resulting union was an inspired marriage of each man's diverse talents built on a bedrock of mutual trust.

Add then Decca producer Peter Sullivan's intuitive understanding of Jones' vocal possibilities in the studio; only hand-picked musical directors and top-notch repertoire, much of it made-to-measure. These elements combined to create and sustain the UK's first solo superstar, nicknamed 'The Tiger' . . .

The Nashville Teens

They identified with rock 'n' roll stars all right, in the Sixties backing Jerry Lee, Carl Perkins and Bo Diddley as they circuited the dancehalls. The Nashville Teens though were a powerful R&B outfit in their own right who gained swift cross-continent applause in 1964 with John D. Loudermilk's *Tobacco Road* (UK: No. 6; US: No. 14). Unfortunately, it was all downhill sales-wise from then on.

Eccentric American writer J.D.L.'s *12 Sides Of . . .* long-player also supplied their successor, *Google Eye* (UK: No. 10) – about a fish – and way-back-then twin lead singers Ray Phillips and Arthur Sharp, John Hawken (piano), John Allen (guitar), Pete Shannon (bass) and Barry Jenkins (drums) insisted their next ten top decks might come from the same carbon pellet. They didn't.

Produced initially by Mickie Most, 1966's *The Hard Way* (No. 45) was their final chart admission, meaning later superb efforts withered and died.

At least the Teens slipped on to cinema screens twice in 1965. The movies? *Be My Guest* and *Pop Gear* (aka *Go Go Mania*).

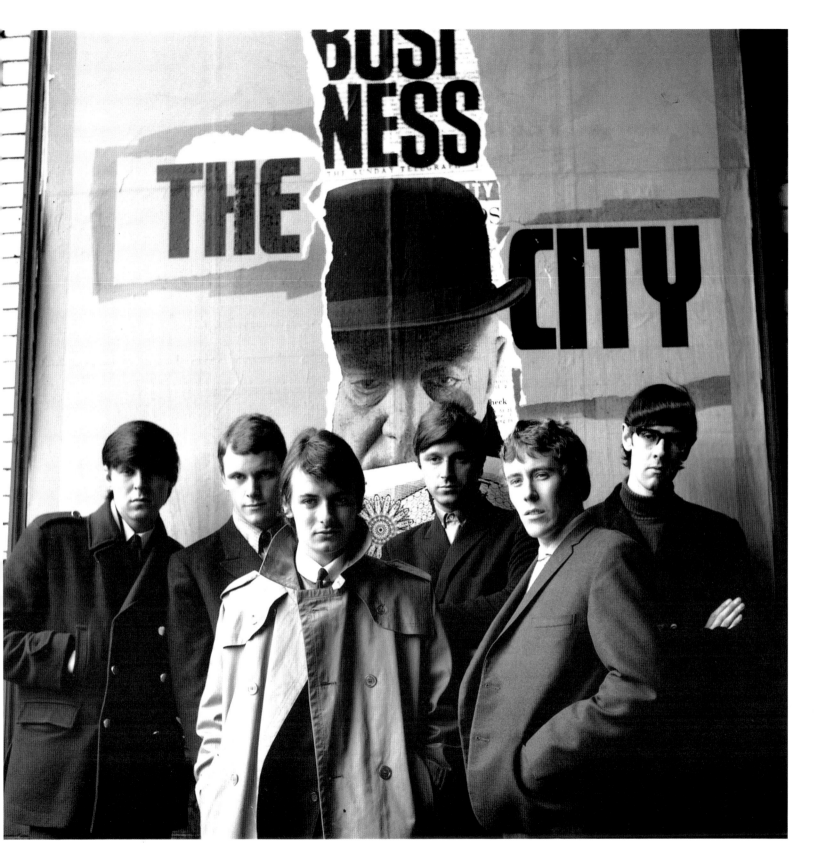

Marianne Faithfull

Within weeks of meeting Marianne Faithfull at a party in 1964, he who was guiding the exploits of the Rolling Stones, Andrew Oldham, presented the striking blonde singing *As Tears Go By* – 'a song with brick walls all around it, high windows and no sex'. Loog had co-written the lachrymose ballad with Messrs Jagger and Richard(s); its universal appeal twinned with her sheer visual beauty ensured instant triumph.

The daughter of Austro-Hungarian Baroness Erisso, Eva Sacher-Masoch, and professor of Italian Renaissance studies Dr Robert Glynn Faithfull, Hampstead, London-born convent-educated Marianne favoured folk, but her gentle, plaintive voice could be heard simultaneously promoting both that and pure pop styles through Decca adopting an unheard of tack: issuing two debut albums at once. Both charted.

A mere five years later her label farewell was as far as one could get from *Tears*, the painful part-self-scripted drug anthem 'flip', *Sister Morphine*. Life was going horribly wrong; today, as its 'A' Side wished, she's found that *Something Better . . .*

The Everly Brothers

One of the popular music's most influential contributors ever, Don (left) and Phil Everly were child stars in their parents' radio shows before setting off to Country's nerve centre, Nashville.

Columbia (CBS) tried one single in February 1956, but after their father, Ike, had his old friend Chet Atkins intervene, they were signed by a major publisher who, in turn, convinced New York's Cadence label to put them on the roster.

Owner Archie Bleyer had the Everlys tape a song by husband and wife team Boudleaux and Felice Bryant, *Bye Bye Love*, which, far from cutting straight country, the boys attacked with twin acoustic guitars, close harmony vocals and ladled in generous helpings of hillbilly and rock elements. An immediate global million-seller, it was their first of many teen-problematicals; the Bryant's had a hand in most.

Switching to Warner Brothers in 1960, the brothers' self-scripted *Cathy's Clown* immediately moved three million copies although, for some time, their new output was challenged by previously unpublished recordings from Cadence's vaults issued simultaneously. Decca, marketing both labels outside America, engineered a complementary rather than conflicting campaign elsewhere.

Jonathan King

Educated at Charterhouse and Cambridge, Kenneth King burst on to the pop scene in 1965 – having taken Jonathan as a forename – with a clever 'nonsense' rhyme entitled *Everyone's Gone To The Moon* (UK: No. 4; US: No. 17). Intended as a parody of the current 'protest' movement, it was taken seriously.

J.K. declined to tour, obtaining an English degree instead, though records still flowed and were particularly well-received in Europe. Multi-faceted, he spread into journalism, acquired his own television chat show and produced other artists, including Hedgehoppers Anonymous (*It's Good News Week*, 1965).

Admired by Decca founder, Sir Edward Lewis, in 1969 King was appointed his executive 'finger on the pulse' and brought fellow Carthusians, Genesis, to the label – whom he wished to mould along Bee Gees lines – before concentrating on one-off singles leased to various companies. Most were performed by Jonathan under pseudonyms.

In 1972, via Lewis's major set-up, he launched his own UK imprint, and introduced 10 cc, folding it some five years on to pursue alternative pastimes once more. Outspoken, there's still no keeping him quiet . . .

Them

They took their name from a 1950s horror film of programme makeweight 'B' design, did Them. Known locally as Belfast's Rolling Stones, this uncompromising rhythm and blues crew plugged in at the neighbourhood's Maritime Hotel. It became home; their club, and a personal manager soon followed.

He shipped his five protégés to London in 1964, but personnel stability had no part in Them's lifestyle, and even *during* their first seven-track session for Decca on 5 July outside players were engaged, including guitarist Jimmy Page (inevitably . . .).

Pictured here is just one short-lived line-up: (left to right) Billy Harrison (lead guitar), Alan Henderson (bass), leader Van Morrison (vocals, saxophone), Peter Bardens (keyboards) – pre-Camel – and Pat McAuley (drums).

Them's second single, *Baby Please Don't Go* (coupled with Morrison's *Gloria*) put them on the map (UK: No. 10); American Bert Berns' authored/produced *Here Comes The Night* (UK: No. 2; US: No. 24) consolidated the position, but despite further victories across the Atlantic general dissatisfaction with everything caused Van to cry 'Enough' in mid-1966. Embankment brass hats did likewise.

Small Faces

As the Who were West London's mid-Sixties 'Mod' heroes – albeit a somewhat contrived image – so the Small Faces (a 'The' never actually was part of their stickering) held the Eastern 'manor'. Ultra-snappy dressers, they were the genuine article.

Futile attempts were made to get the bands to denigrate each other in the press. Pointless, they were actually mates and years later individual members would swap notes. However . . .

As an entity those with cherubic visages came together in mid-1965 when former child actor Steve Marriott (guitar, vocals – left) and organist Jimmy Winston (second from right), of the Frantics, threw in their lot with the bass/vocals of Ronnie 'Plonk' Lane (second from left) and skin-beater Kenn(e)y Jones, recently of the Pioneers.

Instant crowd-pleasers, a capital club one-nighter became five weeks; an agent signed them without even seeing/hearing their music; Decca put out the red carpet. A prompt hit with *What'cha Gonna Do About It*, was followed by Winston's departure and Ian McLagen's recruitment. *All Or Nothing* supplied a No. 1 (1966), but Andy Oldham's Immediate snaffled them a year later.

Sony & Cher with Jimmy Savile

Their Bohemian dress sense and unadulterated preaching of love, singing while gazing into each other's eyes, aided and abetted by a wonderfully catchy song, *I Got You Babe*, had Detroit's Salvatore Philip Bono (Sonny) and his spouse, Cherilyn Sarkasian LaPierre (there are several alternative spellings, let's call her Cher), a 'Sunshine Stater' of Cherokee Indian/Armenian descent, providing their own international global soul-warming in 1965. Signed to the Atlantic/Atco combine, Decca's long-term association with the 1947-instigated Herb Abramson/Ahmet Ertegun labels gave them lucrative title outside America.

S. and C. met in 1963 and married on 27 October the next year; the patter of anything-but-tiny hits soon followed, performed collectively and individually, many of them inked by Sonny, though the subject matter progressively hardened.

Divorcing a decade later, Bono purchased a restaurant in Palm Springs, and in 1988 became the desert town's mayor; his ex has since collected movie silverware and become one of the raunchiest female rockers around. How times change.

I think you recognize the 'aggressor' with cigar . . . ?

Marc Bolan

Even from the contents of his first Decca-constructed press biography one somehow sensed that Marc Bolan was visualized as a special somebody; it didn't just regurgitate the usual height, weight, ambition, favourite food *et al.* standard details of the period, mentioning instead a Parisian sabbatical with a sorcerer, cat and owl.

Having metamorphosized from Toby Tyler, Mod, to Marc Bolan, Dylan-inspired mystical folkie, Decca clearly envisaged a possible contender for Donovan's throne in the making, and the elfin youth with his oblique self-penned opuses was taken on board mid-1965, a single, *The Wizard*, seeking converts from November.

Despite his obvious girl appeal and an airing for the number on *Ready Steady Go!*, both it and a follow-up sank without trace, so Decca and prodigy parted company. Helen Shapiro's childhood friend then moved to EMI's Parlophone arm without success but, in glitz and glamour mode, Marc found the following decade highly accommodating to both his musical and image aspirations, until a horrific September 1977 motor accident silenced the '20th Century Boy' forever.

The Birds

They're, arguably, best-remembered today for slapping seven writs against loss of work and earnings on Jim (later Roger) McGuinn's American Byrds as they arrived in England to tour on 7 August 1965, which is a pity because our own B-i-r-d-s's were a confident R&B/soul aggregation.

Formed in 1964 by Alistair McKenzie (vocals), Ronnie Wood/Tony Munroe (guitars, vocals), Kim Gardner (bass, vocals) and Pete McDaniels (drums), Decca listed their opening single, Wood's *You're On My Mind*, on dealer issue sheets for 20 November. It didn't percolate, but the next issue on 30 April 1965, a cover of Motown songwriter/singer Eddie Holland's *Leaving Here*, grazed the Top 50, at No. 45, assisted – or maybe hindered – by a TV slot gimmick during which the quintet were raised and lowered on wires.

One more autochanger-candidate at Decca, one on Reaction a year later; a bit-part in a horror movie, *The Deadly Bees* (1966), and the flock scattered that November, three quitting music, Gardner (Creation/Ashton, Gardner and Dyke/Badger) and Wood (Creation/Faces/Rolling Stones) eventually pecking golden corn.

Paul & Barry Ryan

Although she pleaded with them not to follow in her showbiz footsteps, Marion Sapherson's twins brought her round to their way of thinking.

Mum, known to all as Marion Ryan, 1958 hitmaker of *Love Me Forever* and a regular with Ray Ellington's Quartet, probably feared that Paul and Barry might get a hard time from some, being perceived as 'silver-spoon-fame-on-the-plate' candidates, but when, at sixteen, they drew applause as unbilled support act to the Mojos at Crawley Town Hall, Sussex, she accepted that further resistance was pointless.

With a Decca contract and a Les Reed/Peter Callander composition, *Don't Bring Me Your Heartaches* (1965), they bounded to No. 13 first time out, though seven further hits later must have finally wearied of still reading agents' 'justifications', such as: 'Nobody is saying the boys are twin Mario Lanzas, but they are natural entertainers and . . .

Pulling out, collectively both wanted respect, individually Paul wanted to write; Barry an image sans suits. Their wishes were granted, *Eloise* (MGM, 1968) the resulting victorious vehicle.

P. F. Sloan and Barry McGuire

The wonderful rasp heard on the New Christy Minstrels 1963 hit, *Green, Green*, was that of Oklahoma City's Barry McGuire; two years later it was prophesying the end of civilization – and everything else – as we knew it via singer/songwriter Phillip 'Flip' (P.F.) Sloan's *Eve Of Destruction*, banned by many radio stations for its negative theme (US: No. 1; UK: No. 3).

Sloan (left), a protest-folkie, was also a pure pop and surf man who, both before and after, came up with the goods for acts like the Grass Roots and Britain's Herman's Hermits. He and McGuire recorded for Lou Adler's Dunhill label – then routed through RCA, hence Decca's involvement – all having initially met at Ciro's in Los Angeles at a Byrds' opening, but Barry was unable to follow significantly such a one-off harbinger and later embraced religion.

Back in 1965 though, across America the Spokesmen opportunistically countered his finest moment with *The Dawn Of Correction* (No. 36). Albert Embankment felt obliged to do likewise, unsuccessfully, the American Decca disc also being theirs thanks to Brunswick.

Wilson Pickett

Like so many of his contemporaries Wilson Pickett began by performing spirituals, and was an equally avid collector of vinyl featuring others doing likewise.

A son of Prattville, Alabama, who shifted to Detroit in his teens, it was in 'Motor City' while with the Falcons that R&B introduced itself, and Wilson displayed a talent for writing in that vein, supplying them with the winning *I Found A Love* (1962).

Flying solo a year later and subsequently pacting with Atlantic Records, the hits began to flow, soul classics like *In The Midnight Hour* and *Don't Fight It* (1965), at which point Decca brought him over to tour Britain during November. *634–5789* (February 1966) became his final 'black (label) Atlantic' 45 before the imprint ended its long association with Albert Embankment.

It remained situation normal though for the 'Wicked Pickett', a nickname acquired, according to his outlet's then vice-president, Jerry Wexler, through the singer/songwriter's habit of happily chasing secretaries round the building during visits, but which could as easily allude to his animated stage act.

The Beatstalkers

Five guys with an unusually natty line in clothes which would be rather more associated with the late-Sixties/early Seventies than 1965; only the tartan provided a clue to the Beatstalkers' native roots – Scotland.

Managed and brought to Decca by the Philip and Dorothy Solomon agency, whose other clients variously included Them, the Bachelors and Twinkle, despite this quintet's popularity north of the border where they challenged Embankment labelmates the Poets and then-EMI act Dean Ford and the Gaylords – later the Marmalade – for title of top band, on vinyl the Beatstalkers didn't enjoy the success attained by other Solomon performers.

Cutting three seven-inchers with silver printing on dark blue paper centres, namely *Ev'rybody's Talking 'bout My Baby* (October), *Left Right Left* (March 1966) and finally a cover of Motown writers Brian and Eddie Holland and Lamont Dozier's *A Love Like Yours* (July), issued three months before London-American's similar triumphant venture from Ike and Tina Turner – they ultimately moved to CBS, thence benefiting from both David Bowie's repertoire stockpile and vocal backing, but still no hits.

The Animals

Organist Alan Price's fear of flying was to prove Decca's blessing, for in May 1965 he'd quit the Animals, unable to face another take-off, and by August had moved from Columbia's 'Magic Notes' to the Beethoven trademark with his own new group.

Alan's old Newcastle pals (left to right) John Steel (drums), Chas Chandler (bass), Eric Burdon (vocals – seated), Dave Rowberry (keyboards – Price's replacement from the Mike Cotton Sound) and Hilton Valentine (guitar), decided to do likewise in February 1966 once their existing deal expired, following a reported offer from Decca of a guaranteed £100,000 for rights to future repertoire excluding the North America/Canada territories. Their existing US pressers, MGM, offered a reputed $250,000 to retain their services there.

Three singles, an EP and album aided recoup, before Metro took them for the world, by which time only Burdon remained of the group signed. However, Chandler had opted for management and, bringing Jimi Hendrix to London, offered him first to Decca, who declined. Some you win. . . .

Hedgehoppers Anonymous

Originally registered as the Trendsetters following their November 1963 formation (left to right) Mick Tinsley (vocals), Alan Laud (guitar), John Stewart (lead guitar), Ray Honeyball (bass) and Leslie Dash (drums, guitar) were essentially flying types then based at RAF Wittering, except Laud, a laboratory technician.

Once transferred to the Fens and seconded to training on V-bombers though, they plumped for the designation by which their winged charges were known in the trade, Hedgehoppers, and built a local following supporting established groups which were touring.

It was while opening for Decca's Brian Poole and the Tremeloes at Cambridge that Jonathan King viewed them, seemingly, as a vehicle to realize his new 'protest' spoof, *It's Good News Week* (UK: No. 5; US: No. 48, 1965), adding Anonymous as he inclined towards the belief, he later unkindly admitted, that nobody would want to know their individual identities anyway. They were not, singer apart, even to be involved with the actual recording process.

Undaunted, the boys gave up their daytime jobs, but despite four further J.K.-produced ditties had already exhausted their upper-stratospheric allocation.

Len Barry

Before flying solo, Leonard Borisoff, professional nom de plume Len Barry, had already sold more than four million records as featured vocalist of Philadelphia nightclub mainstays, the Dovells.

When the six-footer with a distinctive high tenor plumped for the single life, he joined forces with US Decca, making No. 84 there in mid-1965 with the unusually titled *Lip Sync (To The Tongue Twisters)*, but co-written with two members of stablemates the Spokesmen, Johnny Madara and David White, his dancefloor certainty *1–2–3* lived up to its lyrics and proved 'how elementary it's gonna be'. 'It' being a 1.5 million-copy shipment across the States, while Brunswick tacked another 250,000 on to that tally from Britain alone (US: No. 2; UK: No. 3).

With an all-action James Brown-type stage act which kept his highly polished footwear constantly airborne, United Kingdom audiences had the personal pleasure in February 1966 and showed their approval by taking *1–2–3*'s similar successor, *Like A Baby*, for a pram-ride up to No. 10 (US: No. 27), though all later releases were overlooked outside Uncle Sam's domain.

The Alan Price Set

After keyboarder/vocalist Alan Price decided to leave the group he'd formed, the Animals, in May 1965, he journeyed to his Newcastle upon Tyne home town to plan for the future. Within weeks sketchy thoughts became the Alan Price Set.

In addition to their leader, on the bandstand were Clive Burrows (alto/baritone/tenor saxes, drums, flute, double bass), Steve Gregory (tenor sax, flute), John Walters (trumpet, flügelhorn), 'Little Roy' Mills (drums, African drum) and Rod 'Boots' Slade (bass), and this aggregation made themselves available to Decca that summer.

Musically determined to sweep a wider arc than purely R&B, their debut seven-incher, Tin Pan Alley favourites' Bob Hilliard and Burt Bacharach's *Any Day Now (My Wild Beautiful Bird)*, drew both mutterings of disbelief from Animals' fans and disappointing sales, though its main title was providential: March 1966's long-awaited follow-up, Screamin' Jay Hawkins' bluesy *I Put A Spell On You* (UK: No. 9; US: No. 80), opened the door for a string of interesting novelties until the Geordie boy's next rethink in mid-1968.

The Bachelors

The staved area in which Decca's experienced 'pop' executives excelled was that which is now somewhat derisively labelled M-O-R, or Middle-Of-The-Road. In other words, recognizable melodies with – assuming they possess them – discernible lyrics. Peddling exactly that category of wholesome entertainment were the Irish trio, the Bachelors, and during the Sixties they were one of the organization's biggest international success stories.

Beginning as mouth-organ blowers, the Harmonichords, during 1953 while still at school, (left to right) John Stokes (bass) and guitarist brothers Con and Dec Clusky within six years had adopted different instruments, billing and mastered pleasing three-part vocal harmonies.

Offered the opportunity to tour with folk favourites Nina and Frederik in 1962 as backing crew for Decca singer Steve Perry, they were otherwise auditioned, passed, and 14 December's inaugural single, and hit, a revival of Twenties' sentimental *Charmaine* (No. 6) scored immediately, though 1964's million-selling *Diane* really set champagne flowing.

Amazingly their 'sound' was developed by visiting American producer Shel Talmy, who within months also masterminded aural affairs for the Kinks and the Who!

Leapy Lee

Real name Lee Graham, Eastbourne's Leapy 'I was always a leaper' Lee came under the influence of Kinks' leader Ray Davies in 1966. The Muswell Hill-billy's extra-curricular musical activities included writing/producing for others, and singing guitar/banjo toter Leapy duly benefited from Raymond Douglas's *King Of The Whole Wide World*, placed with Decca under a one-off deal in March of that year.

It didn't make headlines for the ex-actor, antique dealer and entertainment manager who'd also once turned his hand to living from bingo by opening an emporium in Shepherd's Bush, West London, but his moment would come when, two years later, he covered an Albert Hammond/Lee Hazlewood number, *Little Arrows*, produced by Tom Jones' manager, Gordon Mills.

It quickly sold a global triple-million for American Decca – by now renamed MCA outside the States – to whose British arm Lee had subsequently signed, although the former amateur school dramatist was unable to emulate that success with later forays despite the continued assistance of Wales's own Midas.

Olivia Newton-John

Although born in Cambridge, England, Olivia Newton-John grew up in Melbourne, Australia, her family emigrating there when she was five. Academic achievers all, among her relations was a Nobel Prize winner, yet from the outset music attracted the girl with the smile that could melt ice cream.

First as part of the Sol Four, then solo, she sang in coffee houses, was encouraged by friends to enter a talent contest and convinced the judges that, indeed, *Everything's Coming Up Roses*, but delayed taking the prize – a trip to England – for twelve months to finish school.

Once here she teamed up with another Australian exile, Pat Carroll, working in cabaret for two years until the latter's visa expired. 'Livvy' remained, and persuaded Decca to release her version of Jackie De Shannon's *'Til You Say You'll Be Mine* on 13 May 1966 – which did nothing – then in September declined the role of *Cinderella* opposite Cliff Richard in the London Palladium's Christmas panto to go 'home'.

Back in Britain she became part of the abortive 'supergroup' Toomorrow (1970); a year later, though, *If Not For You* kick-started a superstar.

John Mayall & The Bluesbreakers with Eric Clapton

John Mayall may have been the leader of the band but during his relatively brief associations with the Bluesbreakers there was little doubt that guitarist Eric Clapton was the main attraction.

'Slowhand', as his previous producer, Giorgio Gomelsky, had nicknamed the youngster during his Yardbirds era, caused a minor sensation in Decca's studios when setting up to play on the now-legendary *Blues Breakers* album by decreeing he could only perform as on stage: straight into a cranked-up amplifier rather than direct into the mixing desk.

Producer Mike Vernon and Engineer Gus Dudgeon accommodated his demands and the protagonists, left to right multi-instrumentalist/singer Mayall, Clapton, bassist John McVie and drummer Hughie Flint duly bequeathed Decca one of its best-ever selling albums whose influence far outweighed even its terrific commercial success (UK: No. 6). All the more unlikely as it spawned no obligatory hit single, Eric nevertheless departed shortly afterwards to form Cream.

Eric Clapton

When Chas Chandler initially approached Jimi Hendrix in America with a proposition involving management and crossing the Atlantic, the affable Seattle-ite's primary concern was, if he came, could a meeting with Eric Clapton be arranged?

Around London the graffiti legend 'Clapton Is God' was daubed on walls everywhere early in 1966. Not a particularly wealthy one though, the 'Messiah' actually picking up a modest, regular £20 weekly as John Mayall's employee at the time the epithet was coined.

Pre-Eric John had taped one album and a couple of singles for Decca when all decided not to pursue the matter further, until young staff producer/blues fanatic, Mike Vernon, convinced both parties that with J.M.'s latest recruit they'd be better off together; as a token of good faith he had the musos contribute to backing Anglophile R&B legend Champion Jack Dupree who'd recently joined Decca's roster.

Otherwise thereafter *Blues Breakers* resulted, John being signed long-term, but even on that very album's sleeve Eric's inevitable departure was predicted; simply passing through, his evolution was unstoppable.

Engelbert Humperdinck

Engelbert Humperdinck's story is the genuine article when it comes to overnight rags to riches – at least insofar as when that 'lucky break' occurred he was piloted skywards in, literally, mere hours. However, he'd spent eleven years pre-paying his dues, several of them endured on the verge of Poverty Row.

Struggling for showbiz survival for over a decade under his real name of Gerry Dorsey, the Madras, India-conceived singer-scribe met with a pal from his past, Gordon Mills, after the latter had ceased working the boards himself to concentrate on artist management, songwriting and production. Tom Jones had already taken off, now Mills wanted a latter-day Perry Como.

Dorsey supplied the looks and voice, Gordon the name and game-plan; after a couple of promising European placings, Humperdinck's January 1967 issued rendition of country classic, *Release Me*, coupled with a last-minute call to deputize for Dickie Valentine on a televised Sunday variety show, finally conspired to reward tenacity.

Triggering a five-million seller worldwide, Engelbert quickly became, and remains, an industry giant.

The Mamas & The Papas

The Mamas and the Papas were a two-girl, two-boy American notion that, romantically, began to take shape on the Virgin Islands' beaches. The idea was credited to New York folkie John Phillips (illustrated), as one he apparently concocted when he and his wife, Michelle, along with friends and ex-Mugwumps Denny Doherty and Cass Elliot (pictured), turned their planned holiday into an eight-month stay that found them sleeping by the sea in tents.

Eventually requested by the Governor to leave, they settled in Los Angeles, met with Barry McGuire, and through his efforts signed to the then Dunhill/RCA connection.

A songwriter of considerable aplomb, John provided a couple of million-sellers straight off in *California Dreamin'* (US: No. 4; UK: No. 23) and *Monday, Monday* (No. 1, No. 3), to begin a run of fourteen homeland chart singles and five blockbusting albums only curtailed in 1968 by the band's break-up through personal differences. A 1971 reassembly was short-lived.

Tragically, 'Mama' Cass died in London three years later from heart failure, aged a mere thirty.

Al Stewart

Al Stewart's widowed mother traded Glasgow for somewhere quieter across the border when her offspring was three years old.

It was in the sedate south coast holiday resort of Bournemouth that Al initially flexed his fingers professionally on a guitar's strings, during 1962, playing lead in future top disc-jockey, but then full-time singer, Tony Blackburn's back-up band, the Sabres, though by 1965 the Bob Dylan bug had bitten and Stewart took to songwriting and performing in the modern folk vein at London clubs catering to that market.

With Decca still seeking their own Dylan, the Scot became a candidate in mid-1966, cutting four titles, *The Elf* – his own composition – *Turn Into Earth*, *A Pretty Girl* and *All*, on 23 June. No tape for the latter pair has ever been traced, but the former was issued as a 45 on 12 August which did little. No further sessions were executed.

CBS (Columbia US) moved in next, reaping tangible dividends by 1970, though 1976's otherwise-labelled album and single *Year Of The Cat* proved the major commercial breakthrough worldwide.

Pinkerton's *'Assort'.* Colours

Samuel Pinkerton Kempe's (centre) 'skiffle' leanings led to an interest in stringed instruments per se. Sighting a German chord-harp in a junk shop near his Rugby, Warwickshire, home, he paid its fifteen-shillings (75 pence!) asking price and taught himself to play.

Incorporating it in his beat-group's act proved a novelty, enough of one in fact to interest pirate radio chief Reg Calvert – already managing fellow Midlanders, the Fortunes – who adopted a similar role for the loudly dressed Pinkerton's *'Assort'.* Colours and invited Decca house producer Tony Clarke – destined for greatness via the 'new look' Moody Blues – to hear them.

He did, they were signed, and Pinky, Barrie Bernard (bass), Tom Long (lead), Dave Holland (drums) and rhythm guitarist/vocalist Tony Newman (second from left) taped the latter's *Mirror, Mirror* on 22 November 1965, to be rushed out on 10 December.

It hit No. 9, a follow-up, *Don't Stop Loving Me Baby*, stalled at 50 and their 'moment' was over, though Newman keeps a line-up on the cabaret circuit while Holland rattles traps in famous hard-rock bands.

The Fortunes

After Liverpool proved that hotbeds of pop talent existed outside London, Decca swiftly despatched its Sherlock Holmes figures to all points of the compass. Logically, Britain's 'Second City' – Birmingham – was high on the priority list, and a vocal trio, the Fortunes, with their support staff, the Cliftones, were the first to be contracted.

After just one single the back-up was dispensed with and Rodney Bainbridge (bass, piano, cello, vocals, aka Rod Allen – second from left), Barry Pritchard (guitar, vocals – far right) and singer/guitarist Glen Dale recruited Dave Carr (keyboards, harmonica – far left) and Andy Brown (drums – centre). Their January 1964 single, *Caroline*, didn't chart but gained immortality as the theme tune of the United Kingdom's first offshore like-named pop 'pirate' radio station.

With natural harmonies they found ballroom work a-plenty, though two further seven-inchers sank. Then on 28 May 1965 Rogers Greenaway and Cook's *You've Got Your Troubles* (UK: No. 2, US: No. 7) proved to be the end of theirs. Shel MacRae (guitar, vocals – second from right) replaced Dale in July 1966.

Ike & Tina Turner

Tina: 'It all happened by accident. While watching Ike on stage in St Louis one night in 1956, I asked if I could do a number. The drummer handed me a mike and that was it. Ike liked my voice, I started out as an Ikette and we married two years later.' So now you know how the 'Ike and Tina Turner Review' hit the road.

The couple began recording together around 1957, pop hits in the US commencing with *A Fool In Love* (No. 27) for the Sue label three years later. Exposure elsewhere came through London-American's international distribution of that catalogue, and they profited further during both the Pompeii and Philles liaisons of Ike and Tina, although only *River Deep – Mountain High* (No. 3) and *A Love Like Yours* (No. 16) – both in 1966, from Phil Spector's label and the last-named not a US hit – ever became best-sellers.

Further homeland switches took them from Decca's grasp, and divorce in 1976 from each other. Today the lady's popularity exceeds anything previously known, while Ike's career – and personal life – have floundered.

David Bowie

Since last he'd wandered along the River Thames to 9, Albert Embankment, Davie Jones had been thoroughly occupied: with the King Bees history he'd planted himself at the Beatles' label who tried out two Shel Talmy-produced 45s to little response.

Next, Pye bit; a gentleman named Ken Pitt proffered management, and D. Jones became David Bowie to prevent confusion with two others. Between January and August 1966 three more largely ignored singles sprouted; however, impresario Robert Stigwood tried a couple of Bowie compositions on his artist, Oscar.

On 18 October 1966, David cut three more songs which Decca's latest label, Deram, jumped at. A deal was signed; three singles and an album issued; most repertoire Anthony Newley facsimiles, recognizing a hit act on blue and silver earlier in the decade. Sales-wise, little happened. They should have known; even the LP's Pitt-drafted note stated Bowie was consistently two years ahead of time. David packed his bags.

In 1969 *Space Oddity* finally put another Bowie in the history books besides knife-man Jim, but not for Decca, Pye or EMI. . . .

The Mojos

Depending upon which member of the group you talk to, the Mojos' piano-dominated UK No. 9 of early 1964, *Everything's Al'right*, was recorded in either an old church hall or a cinema. They all agree the location was Germany.

Last of the Merseybeat outfits to make the British Top 10 and, disappointingly, the only Scousers amongst those Decca signed, the band began life named the Nomads, comprising Bob (John) Conrad (drums), Keith K(C)arlson (bass), Stu James (harmonica, vocals – far left) and Adrian Wilkinson (guitar), by 1963 having added their part-time roadie, pianist Terry O'Toole, to the line-up at Beatle George Harrison's suggestion. Wilkinson quit after one failed single to be replaced by ex-Faron's Flamingo Nicky Crouch (second from right); then came the hit.

Following two lesser placings Keith, Terry and Bob made way for Aynsley Dunbar (drums – second from left) and Lewis Collins (bass – right), but no further chart entries blossomed. Officially splitting in 1967, James circuitously became a prominent A&R man while Collins did nicely as an actor in television's cop series, *The Professionals*.

The Love Affair

When first they pounded the tarmac of London's environs, for Love Affair read Soul Survivors, their name inspired by US Motown/Atlantic/Stax culture.

Founded as 1966 ended, the group came about when factory owner/semi-professional drummer Syd Bacon's son, Maurice, showed an interest in matters percussive and Dad wanted to encourage him. Understandable too; Syd's brother Max had been a personality with top 30s/40s bandleader, Bert Ambrose.

An advertisement in *Melody Maker* landed jobs for Mick Jackson (bass), Rex Brayley (guitar), schoolboy keyboarder Morgan Fisher and his vocalist buddy, Steve Ellis who, after practice, having Syd's transport put at their disposal and acquiring a prestigious Marquee residency, lured Decca marketing employee, John Cokell, and company photographer David Wedgbury (that one!) to see them perform.

Going quid pro quo with Syd, the managerial aspirants landed the band, renamed Love Affair, a one-off at Decca, covering *She Smiled Sweetly* from the Stones' latest album. It died. David kept his shutter blinking; John took the band to CBS and, with sessioneers backing Ellis, five Top 20 entries ensued until dispersal in 1970.

Neil Diamond

After years of anonymity trying to make his way in music, usually on the folk circuit of the Midwest or living hand-to-mouth as a staff songwriter for 'Big Apple' publishing houses, Brooklyn's Neil Diamond finally found two people who not only recognized his talent, but could utilize it.

Singing authors Jeff Barry and Ellie Greenwich signed Diamond to their company, and in December 1965 Jay and the Americans took his *Sunday And Me* into the US singles' upper echelons. It was an auspicious beginning.

Six months later Neil was cutting his own scriptures besides giving them away after Bert Berns' Bang label (London-American elsewhere) put him in their studios. As he crashed listings beneath the 'Eagle' with such as *Solitary Man* and the million-seller *Cherry, Cherry*, the Monkees at Colgems/RCA did likewise with his *I'm A Believer* and *A Little Bit Me, A Little Bit You.*

Diamond has never looked back, having flourished since in several entertainment avenues, and it all began with a $16 guitar . . .

Billie Davis

Woking, Surrey's Carol Hedges' introduction to successful chirping came while employed by an industrial combine: with her assistance the work's band took a talent contest's first prize.

On the strength of this, up-and-coming impresario Robert Stigwood offered management terms, and in 1962 had a renamed Billie Davis play the female foil on his client Mike Sarne's amusing *Will I What* (Parlophone, No. 18), a follow-up to his recent similar chart-topper *Come Outside.*

Decca bid for Billie solo and a January 1963 bouncer, *Tell Him*, raced immediately to No. 10, its successor, *He's The One*, halting at No. 40. A car accident and label switch then combined to prevent further progress despite subsequent slots on both Beatles' and Stones' tours.

Back where she'd started in 1967, and lilting a delicate Chip Taylor effort, *Angel Of The Morning*, Billie's unluckily lost out to versions by P. P. Arnold here and Merrilee Rush in the US, although Spain and South America gave hers the edge. A dance-floor speciality, *I Want You To Be My Baby* (No. 33) then restored the Davis/Decca combination briefly to UK glory also.

Amen Corner

When rumour spread that Amen Corner were planning to return to Wales, they were greeted by the heartwarming sight of several hundred fans marching London's streets in an attempt to change their minds. Fortunately, it worked.

Coming together in Cardiff over Christmas 1966, Andy Fairweather-Low (vocals), Neil Jones (guitar), Clive Taylor (bass), Derek John 'Blue' Weaver (keyboards), Dennis 'Plantis' Bryon (drums), Alan Jones (baritone/tenor saxes, flute) and Joseph Michael 'Badeye' Smith (tenor sax) were refugees from several local groups who wanted to try for the big time, came to England's capital in March 1967 and lived on the breadline for three months.

Crowd pleasers extraordinaire, they quickly attracted a regular following but, strangely, no A&R scouts until Deram's Noel Walker cottoned on. News of the public demonstration filtering through, he spent a week tracing them and, once seen, pulled out his biro.

A rush-released *Gin House (Blues)* went direct to No. 12, its three chasers and album also charting until, like the Small Faces, they evacuated the premises for imagined greener pastures at Andrew Oldham's Immediate. Understandably, Decca were choked. . . .

Timebox

An act which fitted perfectly with the 'progressive' image that had attached itself to the Deram logo over 1967 rather than ever been intended. The Timebox was originally a six-piece pop/R&B unit recording for Pye's Piccadilly alternative that, reduced to quintet status, then broadened its harmonic spectrum.

Mike (McCarthy) Patto (vocals), Pete 'Ollie' Halsall (guitar, vibraphone, keyboards), Clive Griffiths (bass), John Halsey (drums) and Chris Holmes (piano), who were equally at home with blue-eyed soul or the burgeoning psychedelia and most points in between, knew a good title when they thought of one – how does *Baked Jam Roll In Your Eye* grab you? – and deserved more than their five brown and white-imprint singles achieved.

Their one UK chart foray with 1968's cover of the Four Seasons' *Beggin'* (No. 38), was scant reward, although it possibly encouraged a booking to play a Royal personage's birthday party as they were requested to repeat it over and over again.

Yellow Van's failure to move out of first gear in 1969 saw Holmes leave and the balance become Patto, a jazz-rock orientated outfit.

The Flowerpot Men

So this was the situation: two established British singer/songwriters whose syncopations have been covered by a host of international stars come up with a great pastiche of America's 'Summer Of Love' record style. The lyrics are spot on; a prerequisite direct reference to the city where it's all happening lodges in the title. It's recorded by session musicians and the result, *Let's Go To San Francisco*, is leased to Deram. To be certain nobody misses the point, the 'artists' are tongue-in-cheek christened the Flowerpot Men. Issued 4 August 1967, it charts nineteen days later and beelines for No. 4. Problem: now everyone wants an act!

Solution? Writers John Carter and Ken Lewis, founders of the Ivy League, loan the name to Tony Burrows – present member of that group – who employs Billie Davis's backing band and others to perform it with him on the road. Among the extras are Pete Nelson, Robin Shaw and Ricky Wolff (pictured) who, further augmented, become the Flowerpots for three further releases until evolving into 'genuine' future Deram victors, White Plains, late in 1969.

Robert Fripp

Me: 'Love the hat Bob. Now tell me, just how did you begin your remarkable career? With Giles, Giles and Fripp in Bournemouth during August '67 wasn't it?'

Him: 'I was told that the Giles brothers had left their group and were looking for a singing organist. Since I was a guitarist who didn't sing, I went along for the job.'

Logical. And although it took a month's rehearsals and demo-taping to confirm his position, Robert Fripp was finally in. September saw the trio move to London, where all 'professionals' went.

Delivered to Deram, their quirky oxides proved popular with label manager Wayne Bickerton who became their producer, and in 1968 two singles and an album, *The Cheerful Insanity Of . . .*, which, reputedly, sold only some six-hundred copies, were issued for minimal return. No justice.

On 15 November, obligations fulfilled and seemingly getting nowhere fast, Pete Giles decided he'd rather operate computers while brother Mike and Fripp discussed a new band they'd call King Crimson. There's been no holding back the 'hot-headed' Robert ever since. Wonder where that 'titfer' went?

Tim Rice and
Andrew Lloyd Webber

1965: Tim Rice (seated) is an EMI Records management trainee under Columbia label overlord, Norrie Paramor. Elsewhere in the capital Andrew Lloyd Webber, classically trained but broad of crotcheted taste, is preparing to take his place at Oxford. A melody composer, he seeks lyricist. Rice, one song published/recorded, has skill with vowels and consonants. Approached literary agent who casually mentioned one A. L. Webber. 21 April: Tim writes to offer his services; a meeting is arranged.

1967: The pair assemble end-of-term entertainment, *Joseph And The Amazing Technicolor Dreamcoat*.

1 March 1968: It is performed by a choir and group; May: a larger production takes place at Central Hall, Westminster; July: Decca commission, ironically, Norrie Paramor to execute a professional recording to be issued 1 January; September: its protagonists cut a single for the label, *Sara's Gone To Dorset/Where's The Door*. It remains in the vaults.

1971: *Joseph*'s finest moments yet to come. A new Rice–Lloyd Webber collaboration, *Jesus Christ Superstar*'s triumph signals the 'birth' of the most successful musical-theatre partnership in history.

Clothes by Take Six.

Clyde McPhatter

Owner of one of Fifties' R&B's most innovative sets of pipes, Clyde McPhatter's recordings for Atlantic – initially as leader of the Drifters and then solo – had long been lucratively accessed by Decca via London-American, although they had had little actual published Hit Parade action to reflect this success.

His post-1958 moves to alternative labels with whom they had no agreements kept the North Carolina buttermilk-lover's extravaganzas from the Embankment's marketing incentives, but once the automatic US Hot 100 visits dissolved, within a couple of years McPhatter settled in Britain's capital, claiming he admired our studios' techniques.

Seeing the possibility to regain that they'd lost but more so, Deram had Clyde ink the dotted line and on 8 June 1968 cut three numbers, with a further quartet committed on 1 October. From these two singles, *Only A Fool* and *Baby You've Got It* resulted, with reciprocal impressions etched beneath the 'Big Sky'. Sadly, weekly tabulations remained unaffected.

Returning Stateside when his work permit expired, Clyde died from compound liver, heart and kidney problems in June 1972.

John Mayall

Somewhat different looking from the 1966 model, Macclesfield, Cheshire's John Mayall once lived in a tree house though, as his attire here suggests, a wigwam may have taken over since he was now physically demonstrating the deep interest he'd long cultivated in the history of the North American Red Indian tribes.

Still fronting a line-up of Bluesbreakers that tours the world to this day, although their main man is now based in the States, Mayall's ever-changing backing crew became a genuine nursery for aspiring British blues hopefuls in the Sixties, his accompanists reading like an all-star 'Who's Who'; how about Peter Green, John McVie, Mick Taylor, Jack Bruce, Aynsley Dunbar, Keef Hartley, Jon Hiseman and Eric Clapton for starters?

Never courting the singles market, though several were pressed to attract radio support for their larger brothers, 'the Father Of British Blues' orchestrated an amazing nine chart long-players for Decca between July 1966 and August 1969, and John's decision to sign elsewhere after relocating to Los Angeles was a serious blow to his former label.

Beggars Banquet

Having split with guru Andrew Oldham and strayed from R&B with the experimental *Their Satanic Majesties Request* long-player, in early 1968 the Rolling Stones brought in Traffic's overseer Jimmy Miller and returned to their roots with, as a taste of things to come, the single *Jumpin' Jack Flash* (UK: No. 1; US: No. 3) in May.

This collaboration continued recording from March through June, albeit with a declining contribution from the ailing Brian Jones, and by August had their *Beggars Banquet* set prepared. However, the lads' choice of accompanying cover illustration, a filthy, graffiti-strewn lavatory, did not meet with Decca approval and the package remained stillborn until a company-biased 'compromise' was reached in late November: a gatefold sleeve printed white like an invitation had as its inner photograph the quintet depicted in the final throes of a gastronomic blow-out.

The music was sensational, a US-banned 45, *Street Fighting Man*, had shipped out in certain territories – but not Britain – in August to pave the way for its parent (UK: No. 3; US: No. 5), whose launch party (pictured) was held at London's Elizabethan Rooms. 'That' liner finally appeared housing Eighties' pressings.

The Honeybus

Some years after members of the Honeybus had officially gone their separate ways, at least for the first time, their voices continued wistfully advising nightly the listening ears of millions how '. . . she flies like a bird in the sky . . .', while equally eager eyes simultaneously feasted on their television screens as a beautiful girl in a hot-air balloon drifted lazily o'er hills and dales. Sound and vision combined in sheer poetic magnificence – to advertise a slimming bread. . . .

The accompaniment in question, *I Can't Let Maggie Go*, had been a No. 8 British success, generally emulated across mainland Europe also, back in 1968 for writer Peter Dello (guitar, vocals) – replaced in August by Jim Kelly – and his three compatriots, Ray Cane (bass, keyboards, vocals), Colin Hare (guitar, vocals) and Peter Kircher (drums). They'd put their heads together in London during April 1967 and, through manager Terry Noon, acquired a berth at Deram. This was the second of their six excellent singles here; another also intruded on the Dutch Top 20 and several acts covered their *(Do I Figure) In Your Life*, but fate short-changed them.

David Essex

Unlike many of those featured within these pages, David Essex was already a recording 'veteran' when he walked into the marble-lined reception of Decca's HQ beside Lambeth Bridge: since April 1965 he'd cut singles for Fontana, Uni and Pye which, though good, had done little to raise his profile. Regrettably, this fourth liaison wouldn't improve matters.

The Plaistow, East London-born David Cook, who'd amended his surname when acting to avoid complications with the profession's union, pledged himself to Decca early in 1969. Omens were good. He was teamed initially with the experienced songwriting/production partnership of Chris Arnold, David Martin and Geoff Morrow, whose track record included successful material for Billy Fury and four cuts on the then-current Elvis Presley sparkler.

In all twelve masters were taped by David between April that year and March 1970, from which just two overlooked singles were culled. Their performer maintained his concurrent theatrical pastimes which, eighteen months on, would lay the foundations for further vinyl opportunities also. Once at CBS his first hit, *Rock On*, sold a million in 1973.

1969

Millie

Little Millicent 'Dolly May' Small from Clarendon, Jamaica, took an interest in music at nine, and when twelve scooped top prize in a Kingston talent contest: some trial recordings. As a result, over the next three years 'the Bluebeat Girl' cut several singles.

Since that 'Ska' rhythm was taking off in Britain in 1963, Island Records' boss, Chris Blackwell, whose label was already established in that Caribbean paradise, brought the fun-loving fifteen-year-old to England and launched her. Their second single together, an infectious cover of Robert Spencer and Johnny Roberts' 1956-copyrighted *My Boy Lollipop* became an instant worldwide dance-floor classic, selling some 3.75 million copies, but after another couple of lesser hits Millie – she added her surname to labels from September 1966 – departed the charts.

Tours, film and television parts remained though, and in May 1969 on, perhaps unluckily, the 13th, she cut four numbers for Decca from which one 45, *Readin' Writin' Arithmetic/I Want You Never To Stop*, was extracted. Unfortunately, insufficient 'pupils' attended the lecture.

The Marmalade

Only too aware that a couple of key front-line rock acts were about to be lost before year's end, in 1969 Decca's A&R policy bowed to the prevailing trend whereby 'established' acts took greater control over their recording management destinies – in other words, did pretty much what they wanted and occupied studios for as long as necessary, without interference.

It was with such an assurance that Albert Embankment's powers-that-be snared the Marmalade, a white-hot pure 'pop' act who had pretensions to higher things and the talent to back it up.

Given their heads at West Hampstead, left to right, Patrick Fairley (guitar), Alan Whitehead (drums), Dean Ford (Thomas McAleese) (harmonica, vocals), Graham Knight (bass) and William 'Junior' Campbell (keyboards, guitar, vocals), promptly delivered the single *Reflections Of My Life* (UK: No. 3; US: No. 10), a two-million seller, but, acquiring that freedom they'd always craved, then began splitting asunder.

Five more hits registered until 1972 – including the seven-figure *Rainbow* – but Decca could only look on tearfully as one-by-one 'tomorrow's heroes' quit.

Savoy Brown

From London, Savoy Brown were one of Decca's great unsung A&R triumphs. Between 1967 and 1978 they provided her with fourteen strong-selling long-players which, in total, shifted millions globally. That band did the business almost everywhere except . . . Great Britain, and it was a source of intense disappointment/annoyance to all concerned that the sum total of Savoyan chart action in Blighty was one week at No. 50 – about as little annotation as it was then possible to get – for their 1970 album, *Looking In*.

Fronted throughout – as they are today – by lead guitarist/pianist Kim Simmonds, the blues boys changed personnel more than most, but pictured is probably their best-remembered line-up, from 1969 to 1970 (left to right) Roger Earl(e) (drums, percussion), Kim, Tone Stevens (bass), top-hatted Chris Youlden (lead vocals) and Lonesome Dave (Peverett) (rhythm, vocals).

Frustrated by that persistent lack of UK appreciation, Decca eventually transferred their contract to the wholly owned subsidiary across the Atlantic, London Records USA, where Savoy Brown filled stadiums regularly.

Cat Stevens

When Decca's new avant-garde label was fanfared into the marketplace at home on 30 September 1966, a brace of 45s from unknown artists Beverley (*Happy New Year*) and Cat Stevens (*I Love My Dog*) were chosen as the launch material. Inexplicably, the lady's excellent vitriol-spitting rendition of Randy Newman's top-drawer confection didn't trouble Hit Parade tabulators; Mr Stevens' self-penned canine tribute did, going on to peak at No. 28.

It pushed into the spotlight for the first time a young Londoner of Swedish/Greek extraction whose musical life would display two definite phases, pre- and post-1969, the first successful; the second incredibly so.

His three years at Deram yielded five hits – none conventional love songs – and two accomplished albums, but while hospitalized by tuberculosis in 1969 he formulated Cat Stevens Mk II. Once restored to health he changed everything from image to record company, and found thereafter a new audience who bought his LPs by the millions, but, seemingly, still not himself.

In 1979 Stevens embraced the Muslim faith and became Yusuf Islam, primary school headmaster.